So Cool!

LIVE. LEARN. DISCOVER.

First published by Parragon in 2009

Parragon
Queen Street House
4 Queen Street
Bath BA1 1HE, UK

ISBN 978-1-4075-7883-5

Printed in China

Contents!

Amazing MP3!

Discovery Fact™

One GB (gigabyte) of memory holds roughly 250 songs.

MP3 players can hold hours of skip-free music! Apple released their famous version, the iPod, in which year? Work your way through this maze to find out! When you find the exit route, it will lead you to the correct answer.

Answer: 2001

Say Cheese!

Digital cameras make taking photos easy! You can check a picture as soon as you take it. If it's not right, just take another! Which part of a digital camera stores all those awesome photos you take? Decode the word circles below to find out! The first letter of each word is the letter in the center of the circle.

The casing of a digital camera contains and protects the delicate parts inside.

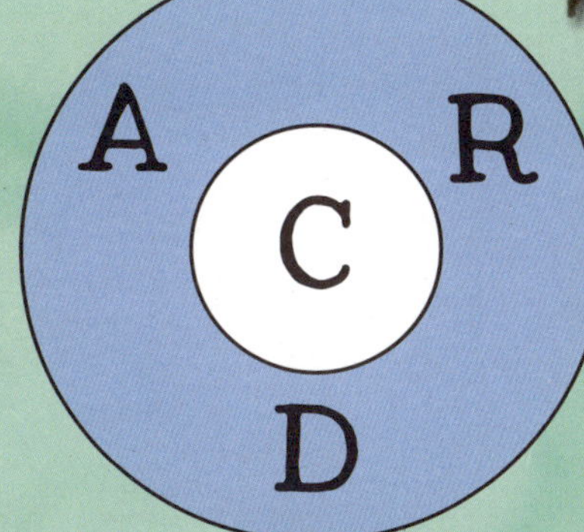

_ _ _ _ _ _   _ _ _ _

Discovery Fact™

Digital photos are made up of a lot of pixels. Each has its own color and brightness.

Answer: Memory card

Cool Camcorders!

Discovery Fact™

Digital video enables sports programs to show replays more quickly!

Digital camcorders are used for television broadcasting because the digital signals produce better quality and sound. But how is this high-quality recording sent to our TV screens to decode? Crack the code below to find out!

a	b	c	d	e	f	g	h	i	j	k	l	m	n

o	p	q	r	s	t	u	v	w	x	y	z

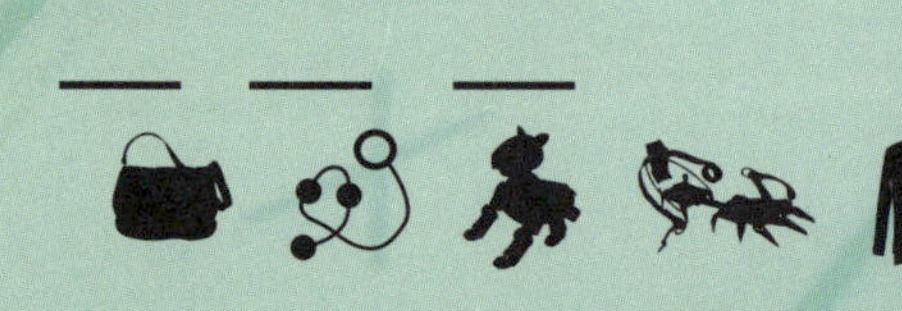

__ __ __ __ __

__ __ __ __ __

Look through the eyepiece to film.

Answer: Radio waves

Snap!

Discovery Fact™

Most cameras today are digital, but you can still buy old-fashion ones that use film.

Most professional photographers use a type of camera called an SLR. It's better for taking high-quality pictures because the photographer can look directly through the lens, so the view he or she sees exactly matches the picture that will be taken. But what does SLR stand for? Crack the code to find out!

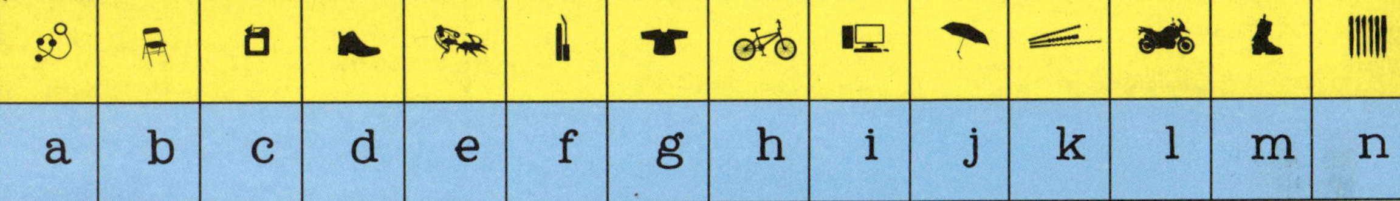

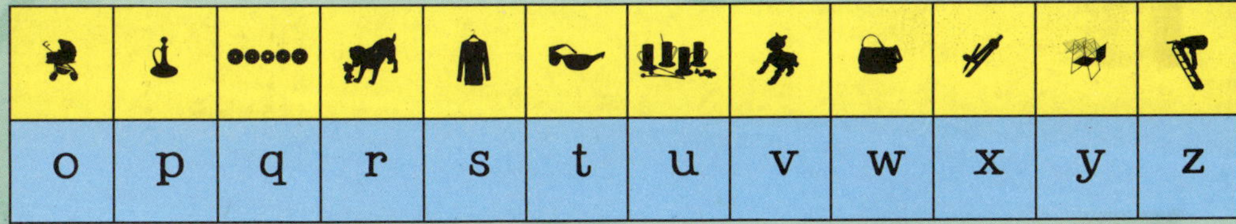

A SLR camera has a camera body plus various clip-on lenses, such as a wide-angle lens to fit in a big scene.

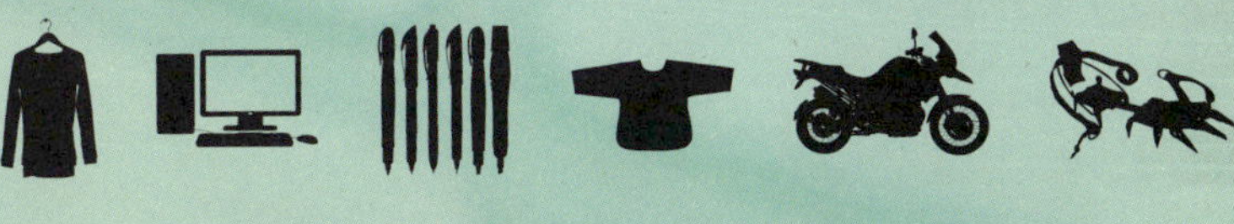

Answer: Single Lens Reflex

TV Heaven!

Televisions are no longer the ugly boxes they used to be! Check out this word puzzle and see if you can find all the TV-related words listed around it!

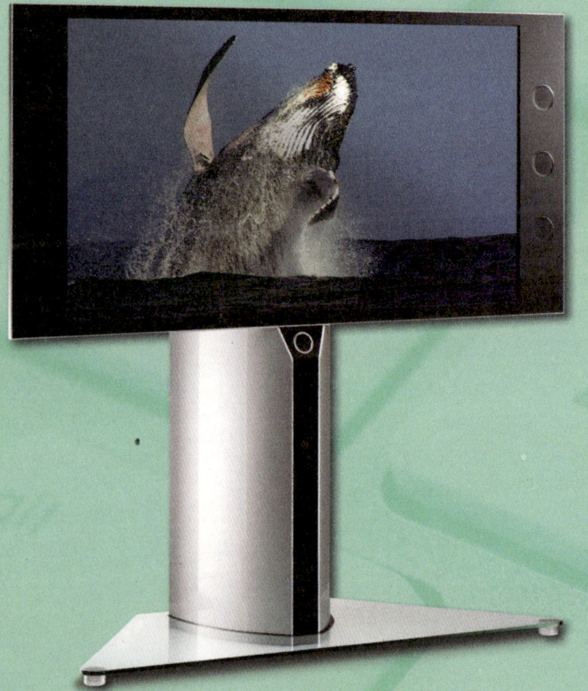

Flat screen LCD

J	A	L	G	F	X	W	D	V	K	O	P	A	X
V	A	C	O	L	Y	Y	U	S	K	A	D	S	W
N	O	I	T	I	N	I	F	E	D	H	G	I	H
M	V	B	R	S	D	Y	N	M	W	U	U	L	Z
A	Y	M	O	W	D	H	E	U	J	Y	J	F	Z
I	Q	A	Y	W	J	R	Y	D	P	V	W	M	F
P	V	T	L	X	I	R	N	S	E	F	X	V	Q
L	O	Y	Q	Y	S	L	I	T	F	L	C	H	O
A	T	N	E	E	R	C	S	T	A	L	F	T	I
S	O	C	B	K	P	W	V	B	S	V	P	L	K
M	R	G	J	W	I	D	E	S	C	R	E	E	N
A	L	L	R	B	L	G	N	T	A	J	P	P	G
I	C	C	R	Y	G	U	Y	D	C	L	B	J	K
U	C	P	E	B	X	D	V	L	H	P	H	E	C

Plasma High definition Widescreen

Discovery Fact™

A plasma screen includes special gases sandwiched between two sheets of glass.

Virtual Worlds!

Discovery Fact™

"Avatar" is the name given to the character you create of yourself in a virtual world!

Virtual worlds on the Internet are becoming more and more common. You can create an "avatar" of yourself and adopt any personality you like! Read clockwise around the word squares, starting from any letter, to discover the names of two of the most well-known virtual worlds.

_ _ _ _   _ _ _ _

_ _ _ _ _ _   _ _ _ _

Answer: A City Life (pictured), B Second Life

Hey, Mr. DJ...

Discovery Fact™

A good DJ can also use the deck to "scratch" a record.

Mixing tracks requires skill, timing, and some seriously sophisticated technology. What is it that the DJ uses to drop one track onto another? The MIXER or the DECKS? Check out the puzzle below and see how many times you can find each word. The word you find the most is the answer!

L	B	H	P	B	F	H	I	U	D
D	E	C	K	S	G	C	M	E	W
J	Q	E	Z	B	D	W	M	S	D
S	A	R	E	X	I	M	I	K	S
K	R	L	A	X	O	K	X	C	K
C	F	E	E	V	R	D	E	E	C
E	D	P	X	E	O	Q	R	D	E
D	B	C	X	I	A	T	U	A	D
G	S	I	P	W	M	I	X	E	R
V	M	I	X	E	R	C	L	F	O

A DJ must always be one step ahead, preparing to drop in the next track. Cushioned headphones cut out the noise of the club and help the DJ to switch between tracks.

Answer: Mixer

Cell Phones!

How did people ever survive without cell phones? Some people send as many as 100 texts, or SMSes, a day! But what does SMS stand for? Find your way through the maze below to find out! When you find the exit route, it will lead you to the correct answer.

People making videos on their phones and capturing events as they happen has transformed news reporting.

START

Swift Message System

Super Messaging Sender

Short Message Service

Discovery Fact™

New models of cell phone, such as the Apple iPhone, have a touch screen rather than traditional keys.

Answer: Short Message Service

Luxury Laptops!

Laptops can be used anywhere! Today, they can also do almost anything that a full-size computer can do. What is the central "brain" of a laptop called? Crack the code to find out.

Discovery Fact™

Heat is a problem for all laptops, so most have a small fan to blow out hot air.

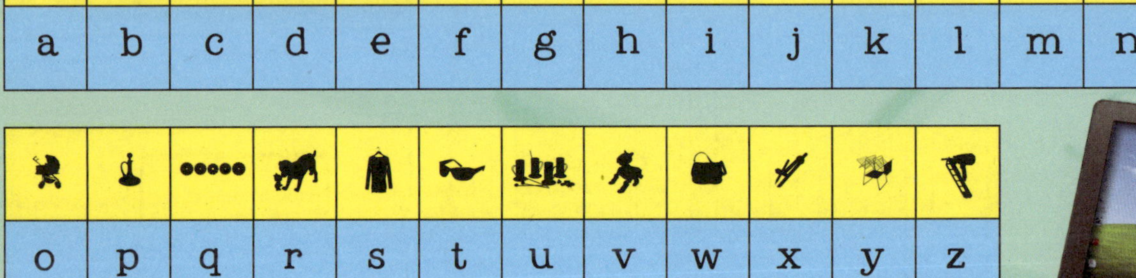

Sony's Vaio laptops feature ultramodern materials, such as carbon fiber.

___ ___ ___ ___ ___ ___ ___

___ ___ ___ ___ ___ ___ ___ ___ ___ ___

___ ___ ___ ___

Answer: Central processing unit (CPU). It is made of several microchips in one casing, with rows of metal strips to connect it to other components.

Wicked Webcams!

Webcams can send pictures and sounds over the Internet to anyone in an instant! The very first time a webcam was used was in 1991 at Cambridge University, England. It helped scientists working in other rooms see when something was ready—but what? Read around the word circle to find out! The first letter of the word is the letter in the center of the circle.

In video messaging, several people link up by webcam and talk in a video version of a telephone conference call.

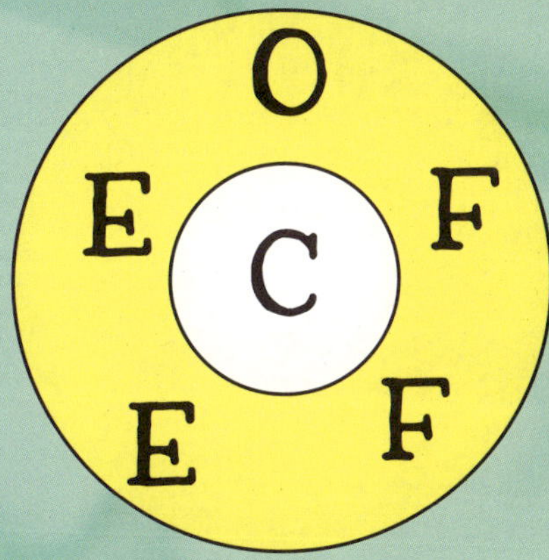

_ _ _ _ _ _

Discovery Fact™

Webcams are often used for security reasons at schools, stores, and banks.

Answer: Coffee

Going Wireless!

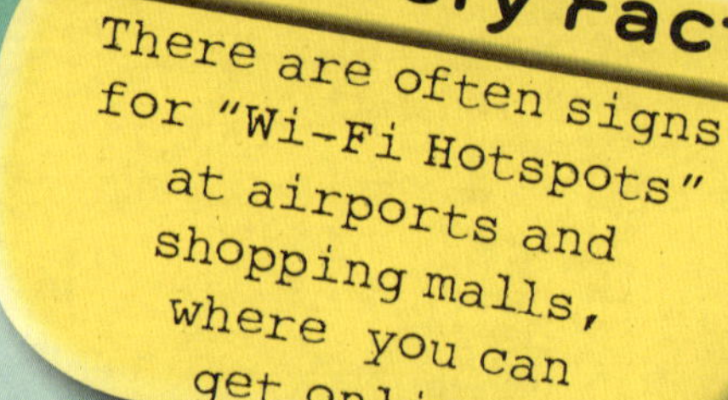

Not long ago, you couldn't get near a computer without tripping over a wire, but now almost everything can be wireless! There are currently two main forms of wireless connectivity. Unscramble the letters below to see what they are.

(A) F I W I

__ __ - __ __

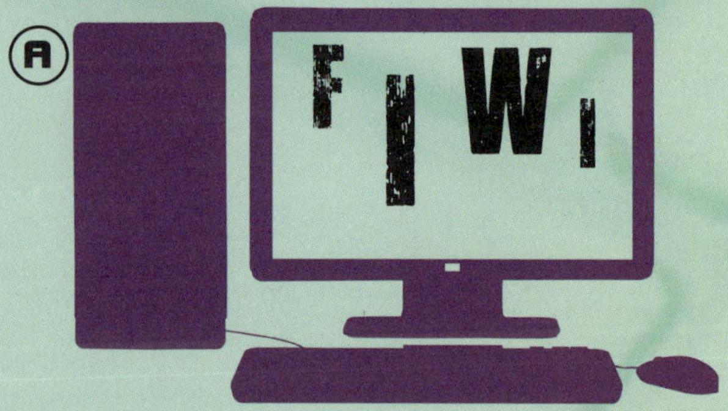

(B) T L T U O E B O H

__ __ __ __ __ __ __ __ __

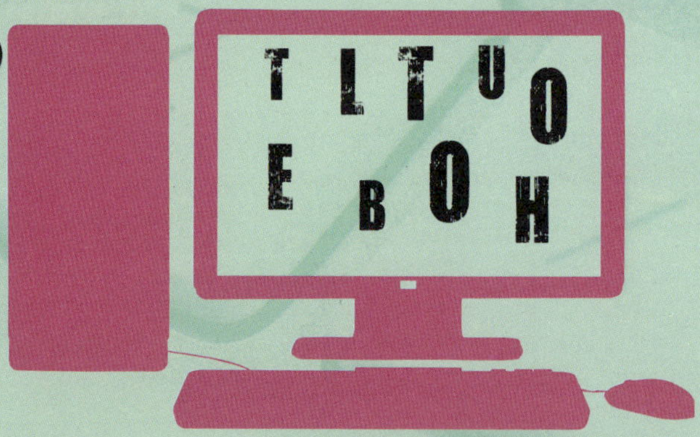

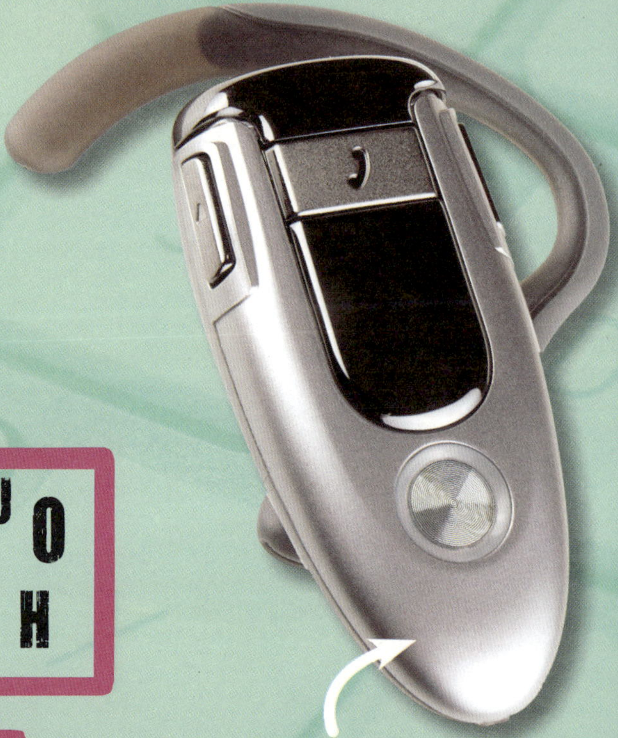

Headsets enable hands-free talking to a local source station, such as a cell phone.

Answer: A. Wi-Fi, B. Bluetooth (headset pictured)

Smart Cards!

Many countries use a "chip and PIN" reader in stores instead of swiping a bank card, because it is more secure.

Smart cards contain microchips that store data, such as your name and address. They are used in many ways in day-to-day life around the world. Read clockwise around the word squares, starting from any letter, to find just two of them.

A

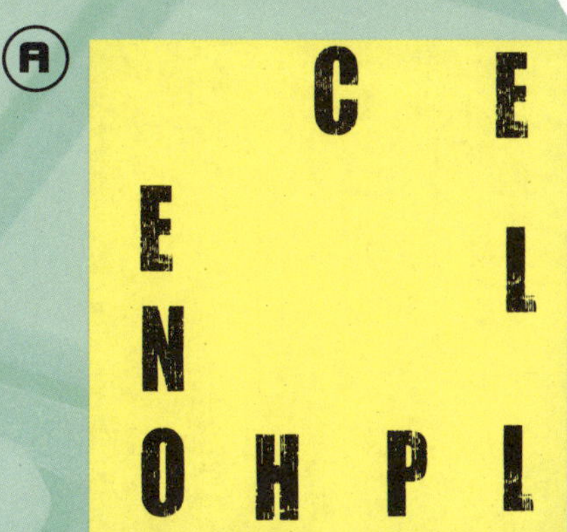

____ ______

Discovery Fact™

You have to enter your PIN (personal identity number) on the keypad of a chip and PIN reader to prove you are the card's real owner.

B

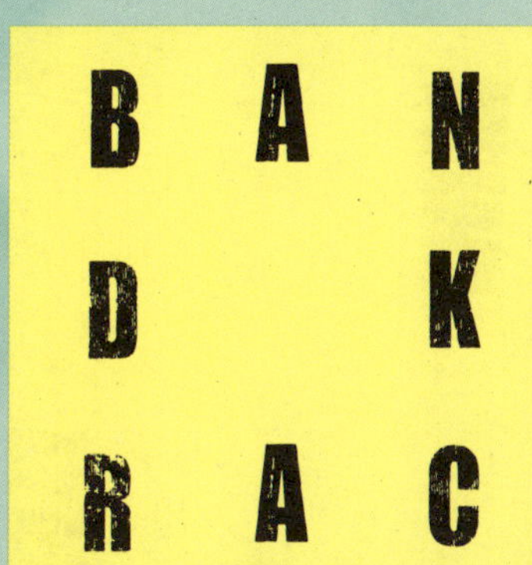

____ ____

Answer: A. Cell phone (its SIM card), B. Bank card

Digital Radio!

Discovery Fact™

DAB tells your radio what station you are listening to and what band! This is displayed on your LCD.

DAB (Digital Audio Broadcasting) radio has transformed the sound of radio. Listening to the radio is now just as clear and crisp as listening to a CD. Although developed in the late 1980s, DAB radios have only been available since when? 1993 or 1999? Whichever date appears most in the puzzle below is the answer!

W W Q V H X V E N
F Q 1 9 9 9 T H T
9 E V 1 H L J U Y
P 9 9 3 9 9 1 1 K
I 9 9 F 9 9 9 W S
3 L Y 1 Z 9 D L J
F L 3 9 9 1 1 H Q
V B J I P 1 9 9 9
E M F T U T Y H P

A DJ's DAB control console feeds digital signals directly into a computer.

The receiver detects the radio waves.

The display indicates what radio station you are listening to.

Socket for headphones

The scan button tracks through radio stations.

Answer: 1999

Surf the Net!

Work your way through the maze to find out the name of the world's most used search engine! When you find the exit route, it will lead you to the correct answer.

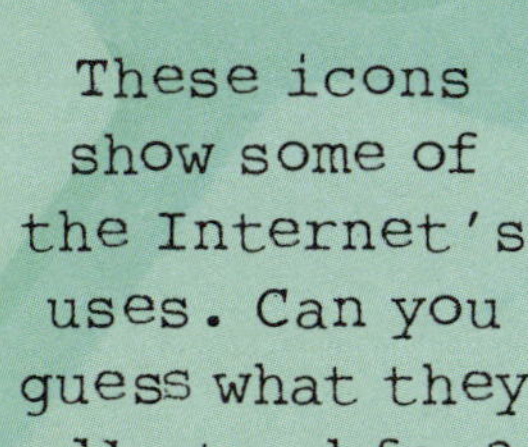

These icons show some of the Internet's uses. Can you guess what they all stand for? Answers below!

Discovery Fact™

The first ever Internet search engine was called Archie. It was launched in 1990.

Answer: Google. Icons (top to bottom) E-mail, file sharing, surfing, messaging, VoIP (voice over Internet protocol: such as making a phone call)

Gaming Crazy!

Nintendo's DS Lite (DS meaning "dual screen") has one ordinary screen and one touch screen. A wireless link allows you to play with others nearby. Do the math below to find out how many of this awesome console Nintendo have sold worldwide.

Answer: Over 75 million (as of the end of 2008)

Donkey Kong!

One of Nintendo's most famous games is Donkey Kong, featuring a giant gorilla. Do you know what date he first appeared? Work your way through the maze to find out! When you find the exit route, it will lead you to the correct answer.

Discovery Fact™

Donkey Kong has undergone four makeovers since he first appeared.

Answer: 1981

Nintendo Wii!

In what year was the Nintendo Wii launched? Crack the number code to find out.

0	1	2	3	4	5	6	7	8	9	10

____ ____ ____ ____

Wii remotes have speakers that make sound effects when the player strikes an object.

Answer: 2006

Get Down with Discs!

Optical discs are everywhere. We use them to store music on CDs and watch movies on DVDs. Soon there will be the HVD, which may be used to store hundreds of movies. Awesome! Do you know the full names for all these discs? Unscramble the letters below to find out!

Ⓐ **MPACOTC CDIS**

_ _ _ _ _ _ _
_ _ _ _ (CD)

Ⓑ **GITADLI SVREELATI DSIC**

_ _ _ _ _ _ _
_ _ _ _ _ _ _ _ _
_ _ _ _ (DVD)

Ⓒ **AOLOGHRHIPC RESVELATI SDIC**

_ _ _ _ _ _ _ _ _ _ _
_ _ _ _ _ _ _ _ _
_ _ _ _ (HVD)

Discovery Fact™

All optical discs are read using lasers. Different discs use different types.

Answer: A Compact disc, B Digital versatile disc, C Holographic versatile disc

Going Green!

Eco homes are made of "low-impact" materials, such as wood, which need little energy to manufacture or prepare.

Eco homes are the homes of the future. They are made from sustainable material and waste less energy. Read around the word circles to find two eco-friendly ways that the houses power themselves. The first letter of each word is the letter in the center of the circle.

In this eco home, large, sun-facing windows trap and store heat like a greenhouse.

A

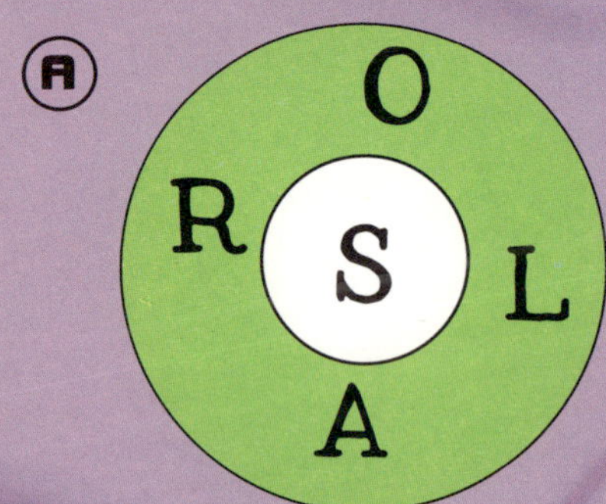

_ _ _ _ _ panels

B

Wind _ _ _ _ _ _ _ _

Answer: A Solar panels, B Wind turbines

Micro Living!

Soaring house prices in big cities make it hard for people to find affordable homes, so a small living space—a micro apartment—that costs less makes sense. Crack the number code below to find out how large the floor area of the micro apartmemt below is.

Micro apartments in a modular housing development are stacked together on site, helping to cut buying and running costs.

0	1	2	3	4	5	6	7	8	9	10

__ __ __ square feet

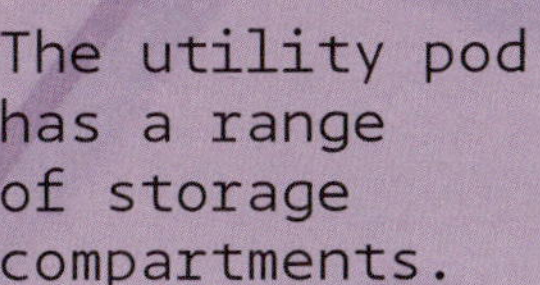

The utility pod has a range of storage compartments.

The large, double-glazed "window-wall" lets in natural light.

The sliding wall panels lead into the double bedroom.

Discovery Fact™

To test micro-apartment life, volunteers have been monitored in experiments by TV cameras.

Answer: 345 square feet

Pet Gadgets! 

The Bowlingual microphone-transmitter converts bark noises into radio waves and sends them to a receiver which analyzes them into six bark meanings. Follow the lines to match each dog translator icon that appears on the receiver to its meaning!

1. Happy
2. Needy
3. Sad
4. On guard
5. Assertive
6. Frustrated

Discovery Fact™

Robotic pet feeders can dispense food for pets by timer for a few days!

This robotic pe feeder is calle the TX4. It car provide up to four meals.

Answer: A 2, B 3, C 1, D 6, E 4, F 5

Vacuum Power!

A vacuum cleaner's powerful fan sucks air quickly into a cylinder or bag. One famous vacuum cylinder's whirling action is modeled on the action of cyclone winds. These are fast-moving, spinning columns of air that suck up objects as they move along. Crack the code to find out this vacuum's name.

Discovery Fact™

The first upright vacuum was invented in 1908.

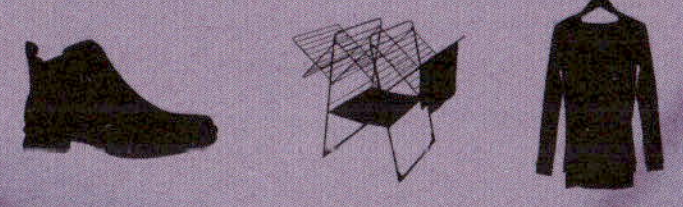

____ ____ ____ ____ ____

The ball-wheel device allows precise steering into corners.

The clear main drum clips off for easy emptying.

Wheels allow you to move the suction head without catching on the ground

Answer: Dyson

Home Office!

Today's home offices have loads of cool gadgets. See if you can find all of those listed below in the word-search puzzle!

This smart pen records what is being written by taking many tiny photos each second. It then sends these to a computer, which converts the handwriting into digital text.

DIGITAL SCANNER
ATOMIC CLOCK
LASER PRINTER
SMART PEN
VIRTUAL KEYBOARD

Discovery Fact™

A desktop "atomic clock" receives the correct date and time by radio waves broadcast from a real atomic clock.

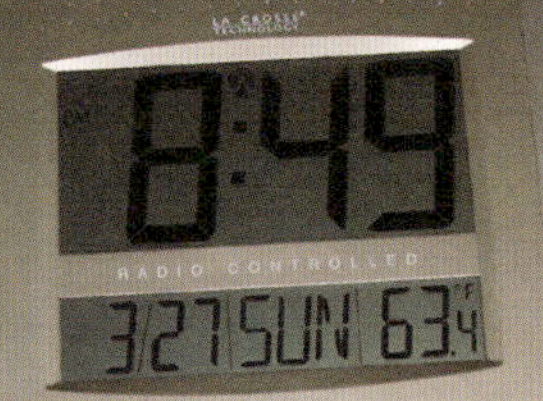

Home Security!

Homes need to be kept safe, and there are now many ways other than the average alarm that can do this. Read clockwise around the word squares, starting from any letter, to discover some home security devices.

A

D	I	G
L		I
	A	T

_ _ _ _ _ _ _ LOCKS

B

N		M
O		O
	I	T

_ _ _ _ _ _ SENSORS

C

	D	I
A		O
	R	

_ _ _ _ _ ALERTS

Discovery Fact™

Digital locks take a scan of a thumbprint for extra security.

Answer: A Digital locks, B Motion sensors, C Radio alerts

Robotic Help!

Discovery Fact™

Walking Japanese toy robot "Nuvo" can recognize more than 1,000 voice commands.

Robots never complain about doing the chores! The Roomba Scheduler robot vacuum cleaner is powered by rechargeable batteries and slides under furniture, along walls, and into corners. But what type of sensors does it use—ULTRAVIOLET or INFRARED? Check out the word puzzle to find out. Whichever word appears most is the answer.

U	L	T	R	A	V	I	O	L	E	T
L	S	C	H	E	D	N	L	E	R	O
T	C	S	C	H	E	F	U	L	E	I
R	H	C	R	Y	K	R	Q	A	I	N
A	O	H	S	C	H	A	O	N	E	F
V	O	E	U	F	Q	R	W	C	A	R
I	N	F	R	A	R	E	D	F	L	A
O	E	U	H	N	X	D	J	P	G	R
L	R	L	D	F	D	B	L	D	Y	E
E	D	E	H	R	U	V	G	A	W	D
T	I	N	F	R	A	R	E	D	B	J

Answer: Infrared

Robotic Toys!

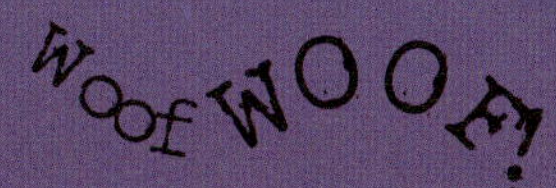

Robot toys are the latest must-have! Robotic dogs are a favorite because they will respond to human spoken commands. How many spoken commands do you think a robotic dog can respond to? Work your way through the maze to find out. When you find the exit route, it will lead you to the correct answer.

START

More than 125

More than 100

More than 10

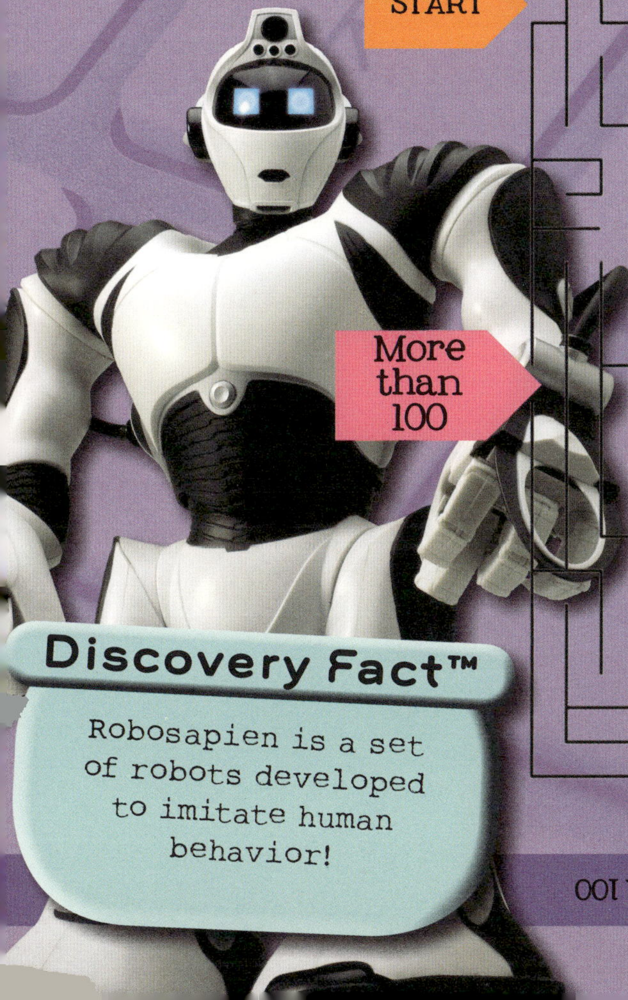

Discovery Fact™

Robosapien is a set of robots developed to imitate human behavior!

Answer: More than 100

Sports Cars!

Discovery Fact™

Only 300 Veyrons are planned to be built.

In 2005, the Bugatti Veyron became the fastest, most powerful, and most expensive road car in the world. It can go from 0 to 60 miles an hour in less than 2.5 seconds and has a top speed of more than 250 miles per hour. How much do you think it costs? Do the math to find out.

(500,000 x 2) + 400,000

= ☐

Answer: About $ ☐

The luggage compartment is at the front, under the hood.

Aerodynamic shape

The front underbody flaps close for top speed mode.

Carbon-fiber composite bod

Answer: About $1,400,000

Cool ATVs!

An ATV is a combination of a motorcycle and a car. ATVs are also referred to as quad bikes. What does ATV stand for? Crack the code to find out!

a	b	c	d	e	f	g	h	i	j	k	l	m	n

o	p	q	r	s	t	u	v	w	x	y	z

Discovery Fact™

The wheels on an ATV can move up and down over bumps by more than 8 inches!

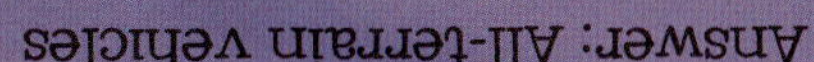

Jet Ski!

Jet Skis are used by lifeguards as rescue vehicles!

A Jet Ski is like a motorcycle on water. It has five main parts that keep it going in the water. Use the letters in the box on the right to complete the words below and find out what they are!

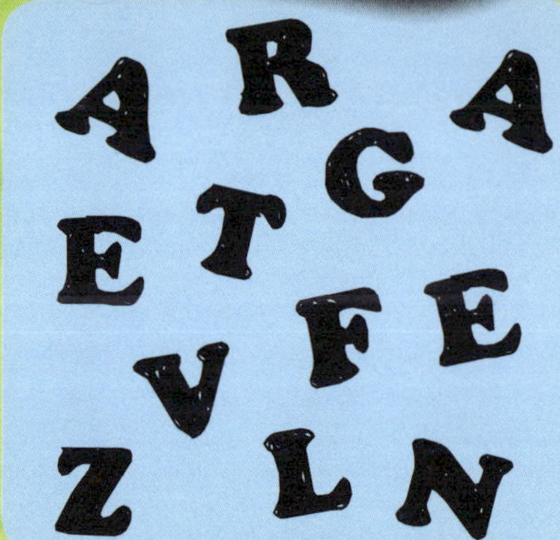

Ⓐ **E_ _INE**

Ⓑ **IN_AKE GR_TE**

Ⓒ **STE_ _ING NO_ZLE**

Ⓓ **IMP_L_ER**

Ⓔ **DRI_E SH_ _T**

Answer: A. Engine, B. Intake grate, C. Steering nozzle, D. Impeller, E. Drive shaft

Powerboats!

The fastest powerboats seem to "fly," skimming from one wave to the next at 100 miles per hour. The power needed to propel a boat this fast is a lot more than a car would need to reach the same speed. How much more? TWO, THREE, or FOUR times as much? Check out the word puzzle to find out. Whichever word appears most is the answer.

Powerboats are designed to "plane" across the water, which means the boat's body, or hull, rises out of the water as it gains speed.

T	W	O	R	T	H	R	E	E	E	T
H	S	C	H	E	T	N	L	F	R	W
R	C	S	C	H	W	F	U	O	E	O
E	H	C	R	Y	O	R	Q	U	I	N
E	O	H	S	C	H	A	T	R	E	F
V	O	E	U	F	Q	R	W	C	A	O
I	T	H	R	E	E	E	O	F	L	U
O	W	U	H	N	X	D	J	P	G	R
L	O	L	D	F	D	F	O	U	R	E
E	D	E	H	R	U	V	G	A	W	D

A powerboat's surface-piercing propeller is designed to be half in and half out of the water. This allows the propeller to be larger and turn faster.

Discovery Fact™

A powerboat's hull is built from fiberglass, which is light but tremendously strong.

Answer: Two

Submarines!

Discovery Fact™

Most submarines are powered by batteries that must be recharged every few hours.

Exploring the ocean depths can be dangerous, so the submarines that carry crew to the ocean bed need to have all of the right equipment. Most submarines would have what is listed below. Can you find all of the words in the puzzle?

PROPELLER
LIFTING FRAME
MANIPUATOR ARM
VIDEO CAMERA
ACRYLIC DOME

A	P	R	O	P	E	L	L	E	R	L	I	M	N
C	P	Z	R	G	R	S	Z	R	I	I	F	A	K
R	R	E	E	N	W	U	Z	A	F	F	E	N	H
Y	O	M	M	R	M	E	A	R	T	T	K	I	X
L	P	O	A	X	Q	A	T	O	I	I	F	P	P
I	E	D	C	B	X	H	Y	T	N	N	Z	U	M
C	L	C	O	L	K	V	M	A	G	G	I	L	J
D	L	I	E	J	K	Z	L	L	F	F	T	A	W
O	E	L	D	P	F	J	V	U	R	R	L	T	L
M	R	Y	I	M	K	J	Y	P	A	A	D	O	R
E	T	R	V	Y	G	J	V	I	M	M	R	R	P
M	I	C	H	Y	P	A	D	N	E	E	G	A	W
V	I	D	E	O	C	A	M	E	R	A	G	R	X
Z	W	A	K	O	I	J	D	M	T	D	C	M	J

Divers use small submersibles as underwater taxis, saving time, effort, and air supplies.

Super Trains!

In 2003, a Japanese maglev train reached a speed of 357 miles per hour. These special trains can reach much faster speeds than normal trains. But what does "maglev" stand for? Read clockwise around the word squares, starting from any letter, to find out!

In 2004, China's Shanghai Transrapid became the first regular maglev train service. It runs from Shanghai City to Pudong Airport, 19 miles away.

Discovery Fact™

Maglev trains have no wheels or rails!

Answer: Magnetic levitation (Both the rail and the train exert a magnetic field. The track and the train's magnetic poles push each other apart to keep the train in the air.)

GPS!

Discovery Fact™

Each satellite weighs about two tons.

You never need to get lost again! GPS devices in cars, watches, and cell phones can receive signals from satellites to pinpoint your location on Earth and tell you where to go next! So what do you think GPS is short for? There are only three complete words with more than four letters in the word puzzle below. Find them and you have the answer!

W	G	W	T	N	N	N	J	Y	V	W
K	L	P	B	M	Y	Y	K	P	H	S
B	O	V	S	H	P	T	M	Q	F	Y
T	B	Z	J	B	T	S	R	F	K	S
T	A	M	L	F	B	R	P	T	Y	T
F	L	H	L	H	G	Q	K	X	Y	E
S	Z	R	R	N	R	H	C	K	K	M
V	U	Y	R	D	V	N	S	N	H	L
K	Y	Q	E	T	C	U	V	L	L	Q
P	O	S	I	T	I	O	N	I	N	G

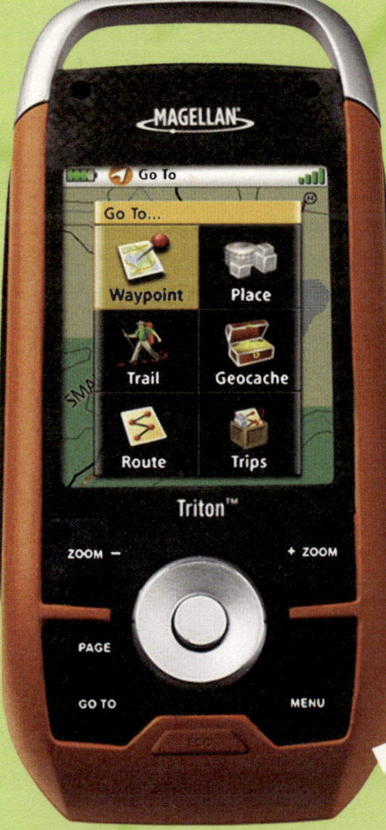

This pocket GPS receive has a touch screen that allows you to pinpoint your exact location by zooming in on maps of different scales.

Answer: Global Positioning System

Look, No Hands!

Some planes are flown without a pilot! Like a model plane, they are flown using remote control signals by a pilot who can see the route through the plane's cameras. Read around the word circle to find out the name of these planes. The first letter of the word is the letter in the center of the circle.

R O D N E S

__ __ __ __ __ __

The Predator is 0 feet long, with a wingspan of almost 50 feet. It has a cruising speed of 93 miles per hour.

Four-cylinder jet engine

A color camera transmits images to a human pilot on the ground.

Discovery Fact™

Pilotless planes are used to spy on enemies and find smugglers.

Answer: Drones

Superwheels!

Discovery Fact™

Superbikes can reach speeds of over 180 miles per hour.

Few machines have more power for their weight than a race-tuned motorcycle! How quickly do you think they can reach 60 miles per hour? Work your way through the maze to find out! When you find the exit route, it will lead you to the correct answer.

Less than 3 seconds

Less than 1 second

Less th[an] 30 seco[nds]

START

Answer: Less than 3 seconds

Ultimate Racing Car!

Discovery Fact™

The controls for a Formula One car are on the steering wheel.

There are many types of racing cars, but the fastest of all are Formula One cars! Do the math to find out what their top speed is!

$(50 \times 4) + (25 - 5) =$ ☐

Answer: up to ☐ miles per hour

Airflow over the rear wing presses the tires to the track.

The engine air box (intake) is above the driver's head.

Tires are changed according to wet or dry conditions.

Suspension connects the huge wheels to the chassis.

The front wings keep the front tires pressed down for accurate steering.

Answer: Up to 220 miles per hour

Hi-Tech Sneakers!

There are hundreds of cool sneakers, all tailored to a specific need! Which famous sports brand has released a constantly adapting "intelligent shoe"? Unscramble the letters below to find out.

Discovery Fact™

"Intelligent sneakers" may have control buttons to select a soft or firm heel support.

Information is fed by a sensor in the heel to a microchip and electric motor under the arch that continually alter the heel's cushioning, giving optimum support.

Answer: Adidas

Wrist Gadget!

Discovery Fact™

The casing of a Sunnto watch has a water-resistance of up to 330 feet!

Outdoor "ABC" wristwatch computers are designed for sportspeople and explorers. The altimeter (A) measures changes in height. The barometer (B) measures air pressure and helps to predict the weather. What do you think "C" stands for? Work your way through the maze to find out. When you find the exit route, it will lead you to the correct answer.

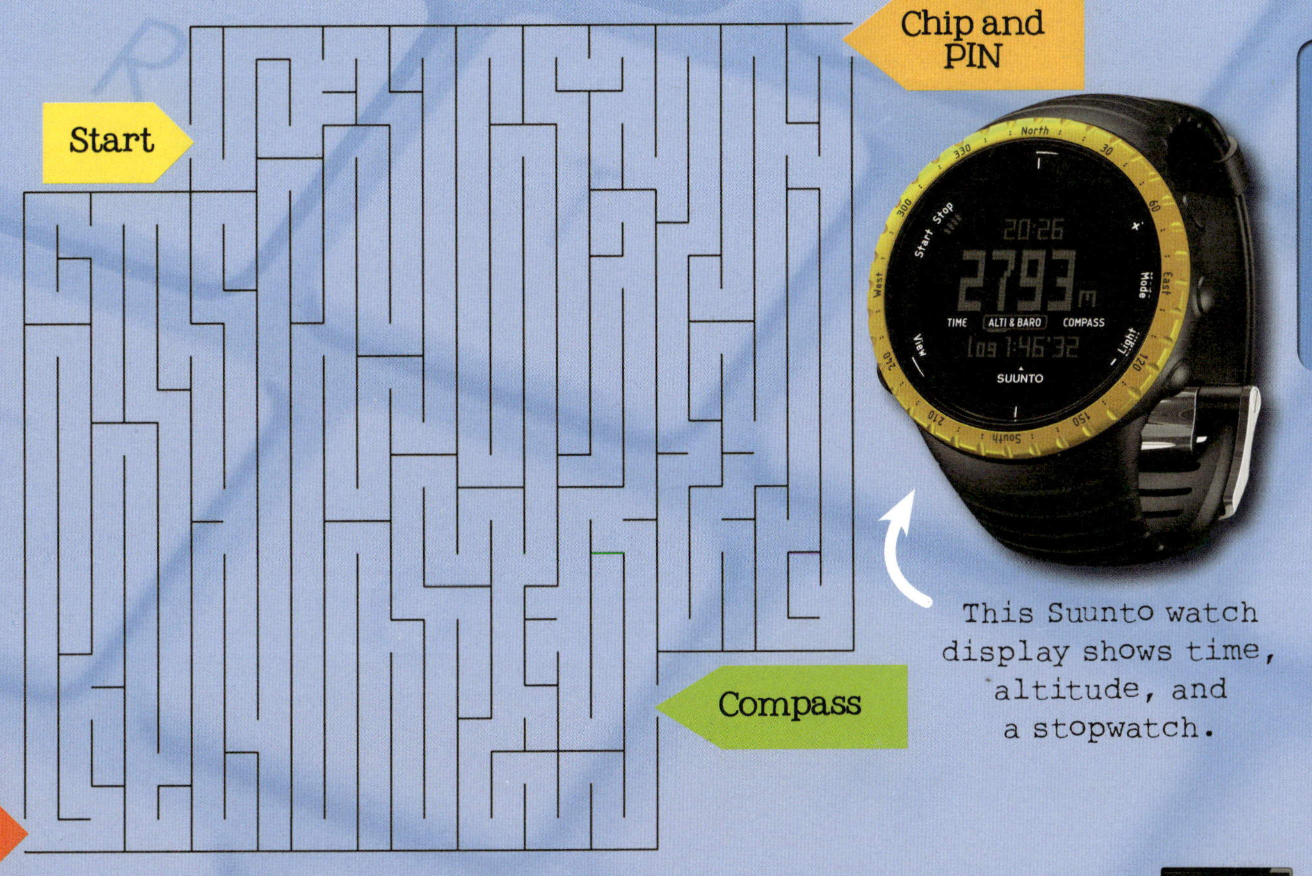

This Suunto watch display shows time, altitude, and a stopwatch.

Answer: Compass

Surf's Up!

Surfers use boards of different lengths for different tricks! Follow the lines below to find out the strengths and weaknesses of each type.

A. Short board

B. Long board

1. Easier to ride but less maneuverable
2. Harder to ride but more maneuverable

Discovery Fact™

Surfers add wax to the top surface of the board so their feet have better grip.

Answer: A 2, B 1

Sky High!

Humans have always wanted to fly like birds, and parasports are the closest they'll get. What cool piece of technology lets skydivers jump out of airplanes thousands of feet up—and land safely? Unscramble the letters below to find out.

Discovery Fact™

Headset radios inside skydivers' helmets let them talk to each other.

This "wing suit" inflates to form a wing shape, so the skydiver can glide through the air, rather than simply falling.

P h a t a e r u c

_ _ _ _ _ _ _ _ _

Answer: Parachute

Electronic Coach!

Top sports people need to keep track of their performances when they are training. What is the gadget called that keeps track of the number of strides an athlete has taken? Fill in the answers to the clues below to find out.

1. What does this gadget measure?
2. In what sport would you do the butterfly?
3. What beats faster when you do exercise?

P

_ _ _ _ _ _ _ _

D

O

_ _ _ _ _ _ _ _ _

E

T

E

_ _ _ _ _

This Polar RS400sd running computer, worn on the wrist, links to a pedometer and heart monitor transmitter to give a complete picture of your performance

Discovery Fact™

Health experts recommend you take 1,000 strides per day.

Answer: 1. Strides, 2. Swimming, 3. Heart. Main answer: Pedometer

Mountain Biking!

Discovery Fact™

Some bike computers now have GPS systems!

Modern mountain bikes are filled with cool technology to keep them quick, light, and tough over rough terrain. A cyclocomputer fits onto the handlebars and measures speed and distance. But how does the cyclocomputer do this? Crack the code to find out!

a	b	c	d	e	f	g	h	i	j	k	l	m	n

o	p	q	r	s	t	u	v	w	x	y	z

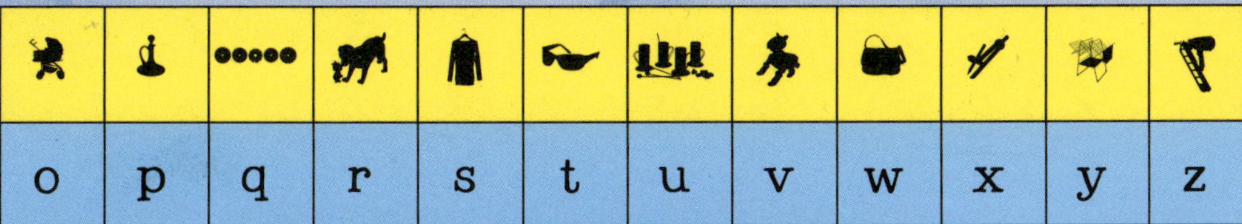

Modern mountain bikes have up to 27 gears, so the rider can climb the steepest uphill slope and then tackle a long downhill run.

Answer: Counting wheel rotations

Snowboarding!

Snowboarding is quickly becoming one of the world's most popular sports. The board needs to be quick, strong, and light and is made up of several different layers. Do the math to find out how many layers snowboards have!

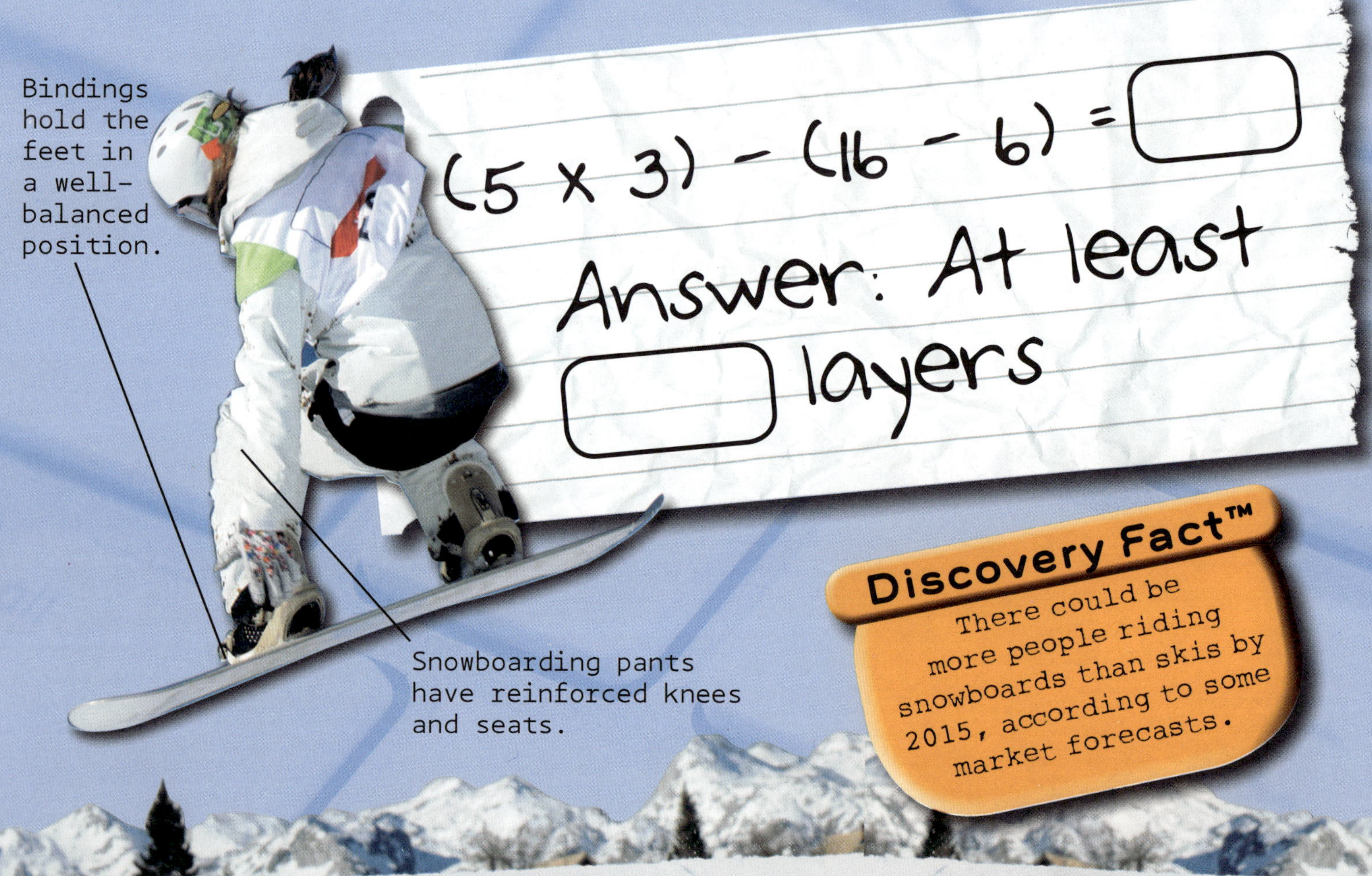

Answer: At least 5 layers (including plastic topsheet, fiberglass, a flexible core made of wood or other materials, steel edges, and a slippery plastic bottom layer).

No Sweat!

Discovery Fact™

PTFE has microscopic holes that are big enough for air and vapor particles to go through but too small for liquids, such as rain.

Certain hi-tech sports fabrics let body sweat pass through them, so you don't feel sticky and sweaty when active. What is one of the most famous of these fabrics called? Crack the code to find out!

a	b	c	d	e	f	g	h	i	j	k	l	m	n

o	p	q	r	s	t	u	v	w	x	y	z

___ ___ ___ ___ – ___ ___ ___

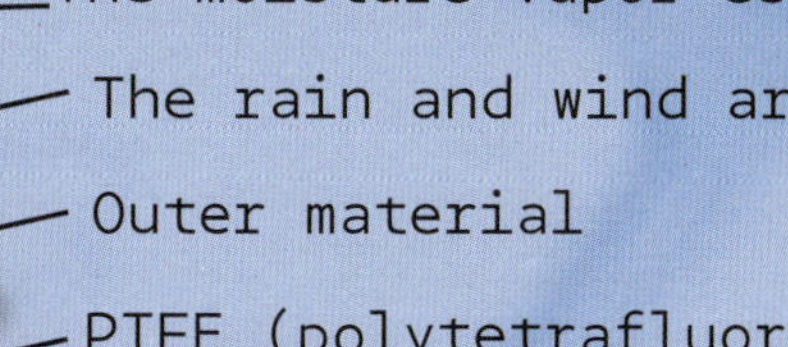

The cloth is a three-layer sandwich, with a middle layer of PTFE.

Answer: Gore-Tex

Cleats!

Players of football, soccer, and similar sports wear sneakers with cleats to help with slippery conditions. The cleats vary on each shoe to give more grip. Some shoes let players twist if a shoe gets caught in the grass. What are they called? Unscramble the letters to find out.

dealb

_ _ _ _ _

tsaecl

_ _ _ _ _ _

Discovery Fact™

Football cleats are usually long for soft ground, so they stick in more and grip better.

Answer: Blade cleats

Protection!

Discovery Fact™

Ice hockey players, especially the goalie, wear plenty of protection in case they hit each other.

Most sports come with some risks, but these can be reduced by wearing the right equipment. A padded helmet is essential in football. It fits snugly so the head cannot slip inside it. What is a football helmet made of—PLASTIC or METAL? Check out this word puzzle. Whichever word appears most is the answer!

I	P	L	A	S	T	I	C	Y	T	P
A	D	F	G	H	J	K	L	M	B	L
F	M	B	W	X	M	B	S	O	I	A
Q	O	E	E	E	K	T	A	U	K	S
M	E	T	A	L	J	Y	Q	N	I	T
E	O	M	T	I	L	Y	W	T	N	I
T	P	N	U	B	C	U	E	A	G	C
A	E	P	L	A	S	T	I	C	S	J
L	C	E	S	C	V	L	N	N	D	H
U	V	B	M	E	T	A	L	T	F	G
G	N	P	L	A	S	T	I	C	I	K

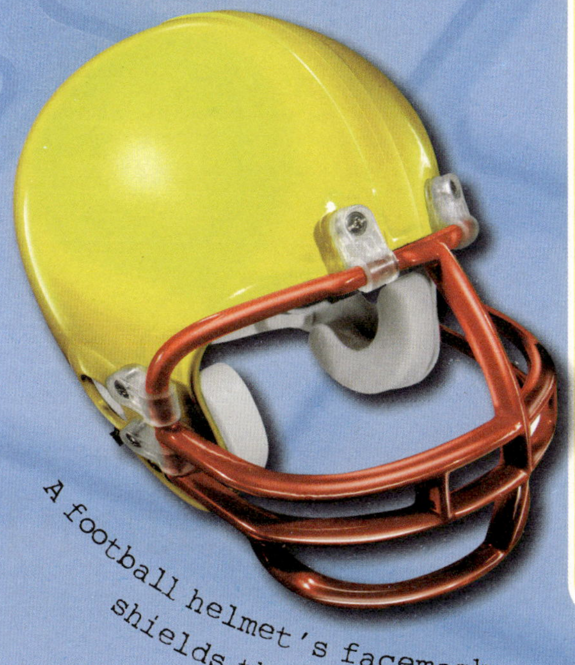

A football helmet's facemask shields the jaw.

Answer: Plastic (a special type of impact-resistant composite plastic)

Electric Fence!

In fencing, each fighter wears protective clothing with wire mesh woven into it. When an opponent's sword hits the other fencer, a light or buzzer goes off. Why does this happen? Crack the code to find out.

Fencing is an Olympic sport.

a	b	c	d	e	f	g	h	i	j	k	l	m	n

o	p	q	r	s	t	u	v	w	x	y	z

Discovery Fact™

Fencers also wear protective clothing, including a woven mesh facemask.

Answer: It completes an electric circuit.

Scuba Dive!

Humans can spend hours underwater using equipment called SCUBA (self-contained underwater breathing apparatus). How long is the typical dive time? Work your way through the maze to find out. When you find the exit route, it will lead you to the correct answer!

Discovery Fact™

The average SCUBA tank weighs about 37 pounds and contains over 500 gallons of pressurized air.

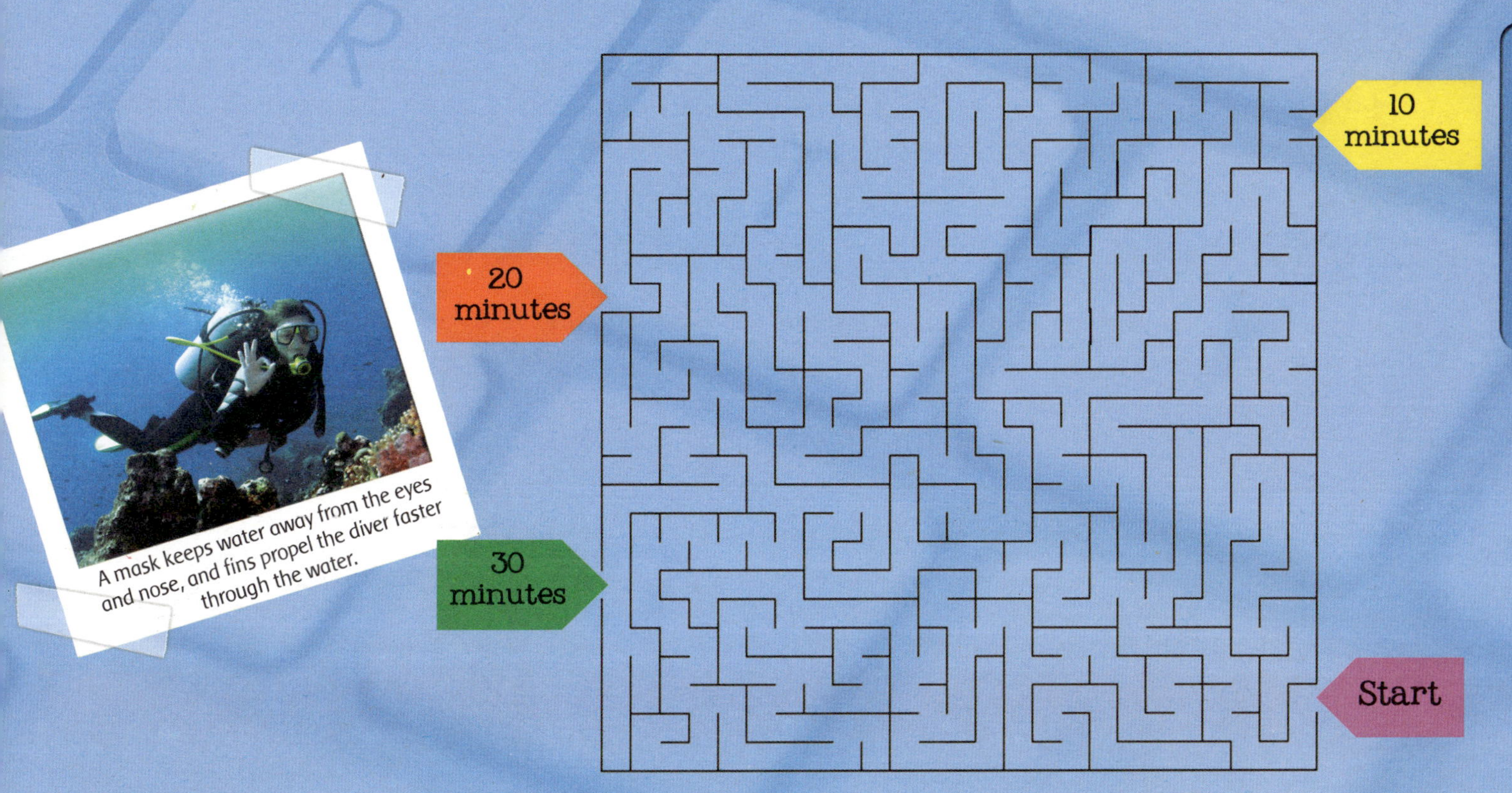

A mask keeps water away from the eyes and nose, and fins propel the diver faster through the water.

Cool Sport

Answer: 30 minutes

Pit Stop!

A Formula One (F1) car usually comes into the pits two or three times during a race. The heavy fuel hose delivers an amazing amount of fuel in a short period of time. About how many gallons per second does it flow in? Do the math to find out!

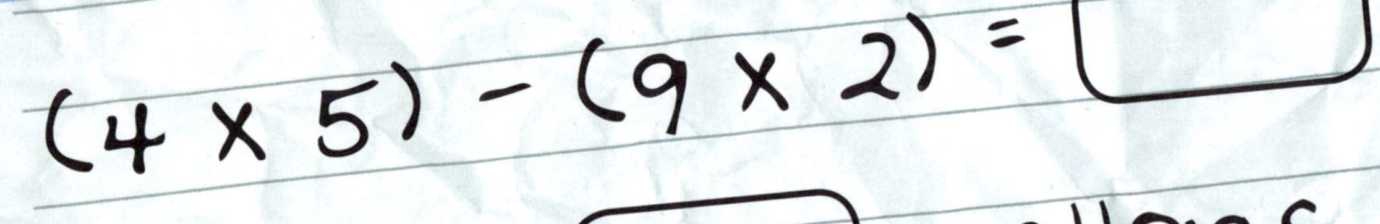

Answer: ☐ gallons per second

Discovery Fact™

A typical F1 pit stop lasts less than 10 seconds!

During the pit stop each of the four wheels and tires may be changed by a three-person crew. Damaged body panels are replaced, and the driver's helmet visor is cleared.

Answer: 2 gallons per second

Speed of Light!

Sprinters cross the finish line at speeds of more than 33 feet per second. A high-speed electronic camera takes pictures, which are recalled one by one on screen. Lines are drawn through the runners' shoulders to determine their positions. How many pictures a second do you think this camera takes? Do the math to find out!

Discovery Fact™

The difference between winning and losing in a top sprint race may be 1/100th of a second.

4 x 5 x 100 = ☐

Answer: more than ☐ images per second

Answer: More than 2,000 images per second

Scanners!

Modern scanners produce amazing pictures of the insides of our bodies. What do the letters MRI stand for? Read around the word circles to find out! The first letter of each word is the letter in the center of the circle.

R
E S O N A N C E

An X-ray shows hard, dense parts, such as bones and teeth, as white areas.

Discovery Fact™

In an MRI scan, the scan is done by putting the body in a very strong magnetic field.

Answer: Magnetic resonance imaging

DNA!

Discovery Fact™

Modern technology allows us to analyze a person's DNA. Each person has a unique "code."

DNA is found in all of the body's cells. It carries instructions for the development of our bodies. DNA instructions are like a language made up of only a small number of letters. How many letters are used in the language of DNA? Do the math to find out!

$(8 \times 3) - (4 \times 5)$

= ☐

Answer: ☐ letters

DNA is shaped like a very long, twisted ladder, known as a double helix.

Answer: 4 letters

Lasers!

Lasers have a lot of uses in medicine. In which ways are dental lasers used? Unscramble the letters in the second word in each phrase to find out!

Discovery Fact™

Laser surgery can reshape the cornea in the eye to improve eyesight.

Answer: A Kill bacteria, B Sculpt teeth, C Reshape gums

Body Technology!

Discovery Fact™

Running blades are lighter than real legs.

Artificial body parts have come a long way. Running blades are designed for athletes who have lost part of their legs. What is the more common name given to these? Work your way through the maze to find out!

START

Lions

Leopards

Tigers

Cheetahs

Answer: Cheetahs

Smart Hearing!

Modern technology can help many people who cannot hear. Look at the letters in the box on the right, then write them in the spaces below to find out the name of one of the technologies people use.

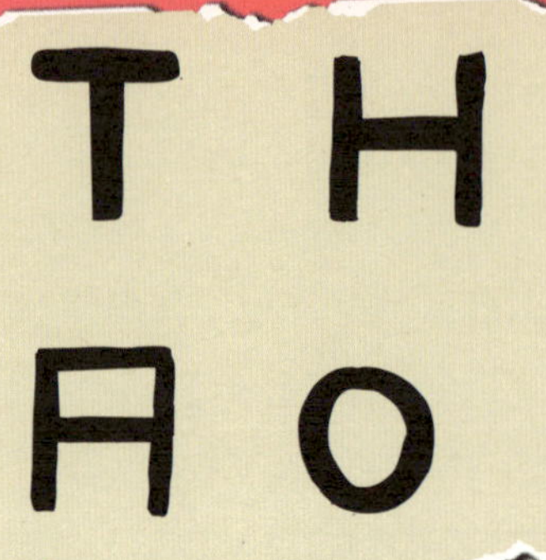

C_C_LEAR IMPL_N_S

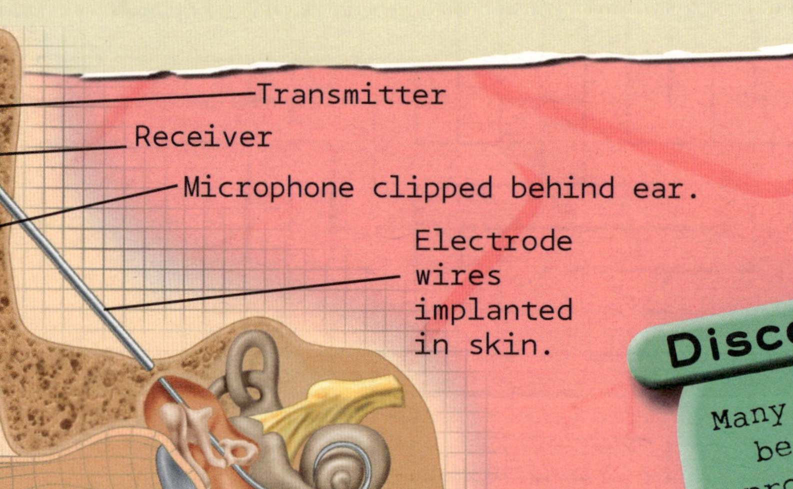

Discovery Fact™

Many people cannot hear because they have a problem with the tiny bones that carry sound vibrations in the ear.

Answer: Cochlear implants

Robot Surgery!

Discovery Fact™

A surgeon's hand motions can be precisely replicated by a robot's instruments.

Some operations are so tricky that only specialized surgeons can do them. But what happens if the surgeon and patient are half a world apart? One way is to use a robot surgeon controlled by remote control. What do you think this is called? TELESURGERY or ROBOSURGERY? Look at the word puzzle below. Whichever word appears most is the answer!

The robot has four or more sets of "hands" with detachable tips. Different tip designs are used for different jobs.

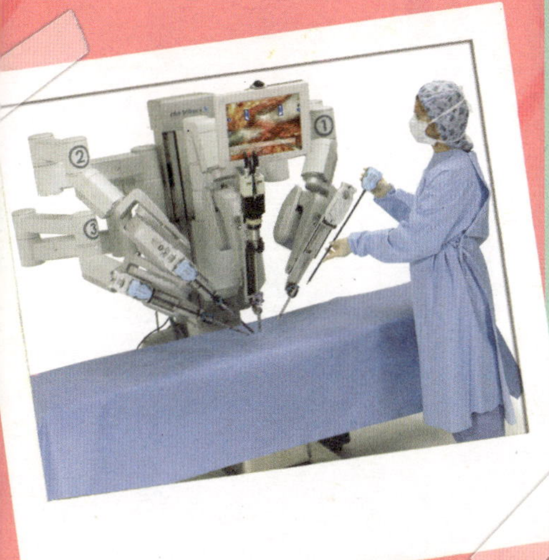

K	R	O	V	T	E	L	E	S	U	R	G	E	R	Y
Q	X	P	E	A	Z	J	B	D	M	Q	I	L	H	N
S	Q	E	T	E	L	E	S	U	R	G	E	R	Y	N
R	Y	R	E	G	R	U	S	O	B	O	R	Z	W	F
F	Y	R	E	G	R	U	S	E	L	E	T	Y	T	U
R	O	B	O	S	U	R	G	E	R	Y	I	I	T	V
O	Z	P	H	V	D	P	I	O	M	E	X	G	C	P
L	T	A	R	P	C	T	N	D	E	H	D	K	Z	R
H	G	M	Y	R	E	G	R	U	S	E	L	E	T	A
W	F	B	P	S	T	A	W	S	E	V	I	N	A	X
I	Q	Q	Y	R	E	G	R	U	S	O	B	O	R	I
O	U	H	V	R	O	B	O	S	U	R	G	E	R	Y
L	U	T	E	W	Z	R	F	K	F	Z	P	V	E	M
D	I	X	S	K	N	G	K	H	C	G	J	N	Q	J
D	T	E	L	E	S	U	R	G	E	R	Y	F	G	H

Answer: Telesurgery

Nanomedicine!

Nanotechnology involves devices built at the scale of individual atoms and molecules. In the future, devices could float in our blood and even get into body cells to fix problems. What do you think these might be called? Unscramble the letters to find out!

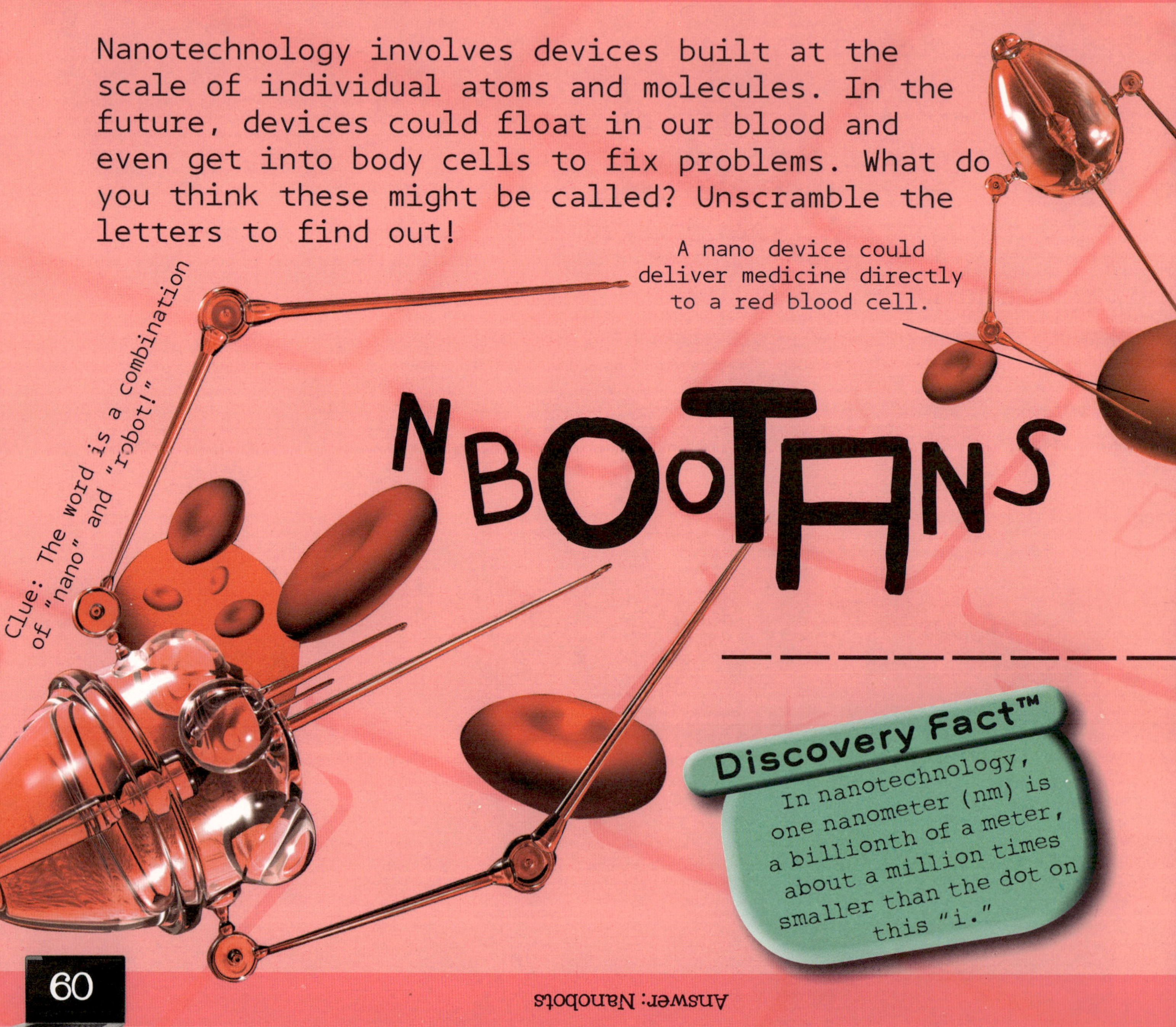

A nano device could deliver medicine directly to a red blood cell.

Clue: The word is a combination of "nano" and "robot!"

Discovery Fact™

In nanotechnology, one nanometer (nm) is a billionth of a meter, about a million times smaller than the dot on this "i."

Answer: Nanobots

Massage Machine!

Luxury massage machines have various speeds and settings, from gentle to powerful. Massages have several benefits. Unscramble the letters in the last word in each phrase to find out the main ones!

Discovery Fact™

Sensors in a massage machine monitor the pressure they apply and adjust it for the best effect.

Ⓐ improve blood **ofwl**

_ _ _ _

Ⓑ relax **lucemss**

_ _ _ _ _ _ _

Ⓒ ease stiff **jintos**

_ _ _ _ _ _

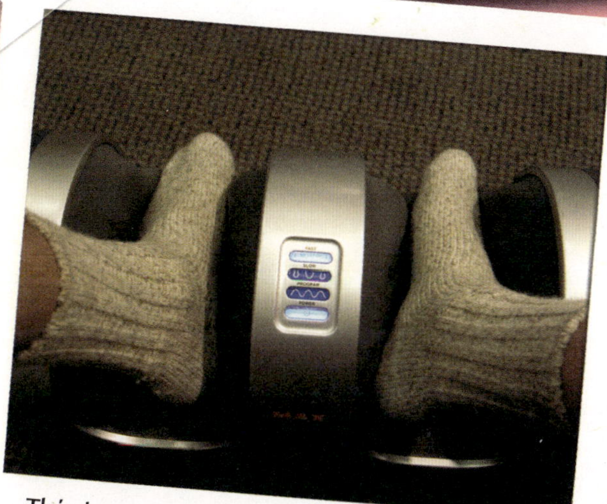

This luxurious massage machine squeezes and kneads the foot muscles.

Answer: A Improve blood flow, B Relax muscles, C Ease stiff joints

How Big?

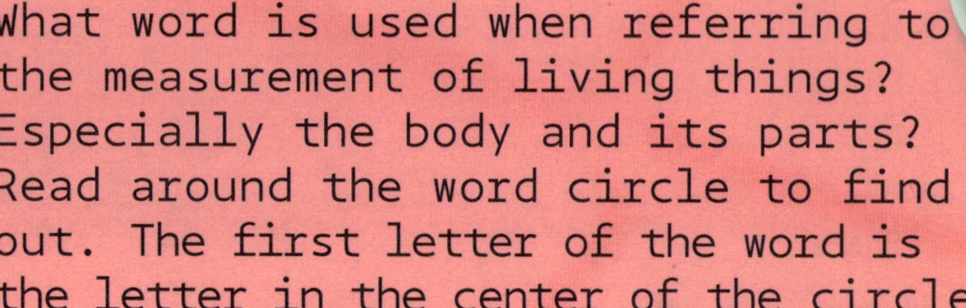

What word is used when referring to the measurement of living things? Especially the body and its parts? Read around the word circle to find out. The first letter of the word is the letter in the center of the circle.

Discovery Fact™

We use the word "germ" to refer to microscopic creatures, such as viruses, bacteria, and protozoa.

Clue: The answer contains the word "metric."

_ _ _ _ _ _ _ _ _

Fight Back!

What does the body use to fight off invading germs that can cause disease? Crack the code to find out.

z	y	x	w	v	u	t	s	r	q	p	o	n	m	l	k	j	i	h	g	f	e	d	c	b
a	b	c	d	e	f	g	h	i	j	k	l	m	n	o	p	q	r	s	t	u	v	w	x	y

Several types of influenza virus cause different forms of flu.

r	n	n	f	m	v		h	b	h	g	v	n

Answer (top): Biometric   Answer (bottom): Immune system

Heart Stopping!

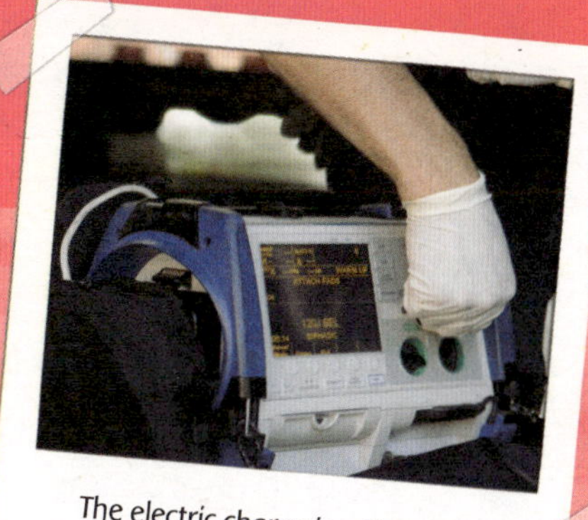
The electric charge is adjustable.

If a person's heart stops or goes into fibrillation (rapid, disorganized fluttering), medics have a machine that can shock it back into a regular rhythm by passing a burst of electricity through the heart. Crack the code below to find out the name of this machine!

z	y	x	w	v	u	t	s	r	q	p	o	n	m	l	k	j	i	h	g	f	e	d	c	b	a
a	b	c	d	e	f	g	h	i	j	k	l	m	n	o	p	q	r	s	t	u	v	w	x	y	z

w	v	u	r	y	i	r	o	o	z	g	l	i

Discovery Fact™

The faster a person's pulse and blood pressure return to normal after activity, the healthier the heart.

Heart Monitor!

A portable heart monitor is essential for anyone with a history of cardio (heart) problems. One thing it measures is blood pressure, but what is the other? Unscramble this word heart to find out. The first letter of the word is the letter in the center of the heart.

____ ____ ____ ____ ____

Answer (top): Defibrillator Answer (bottom): Pulse

Mission Control!

Space missions are managed by a mission control center. The Johnson Space Center (JSC) near Houston, Texas, is the U.S. center. How many astronauts do you think work there? Do the math to find out!

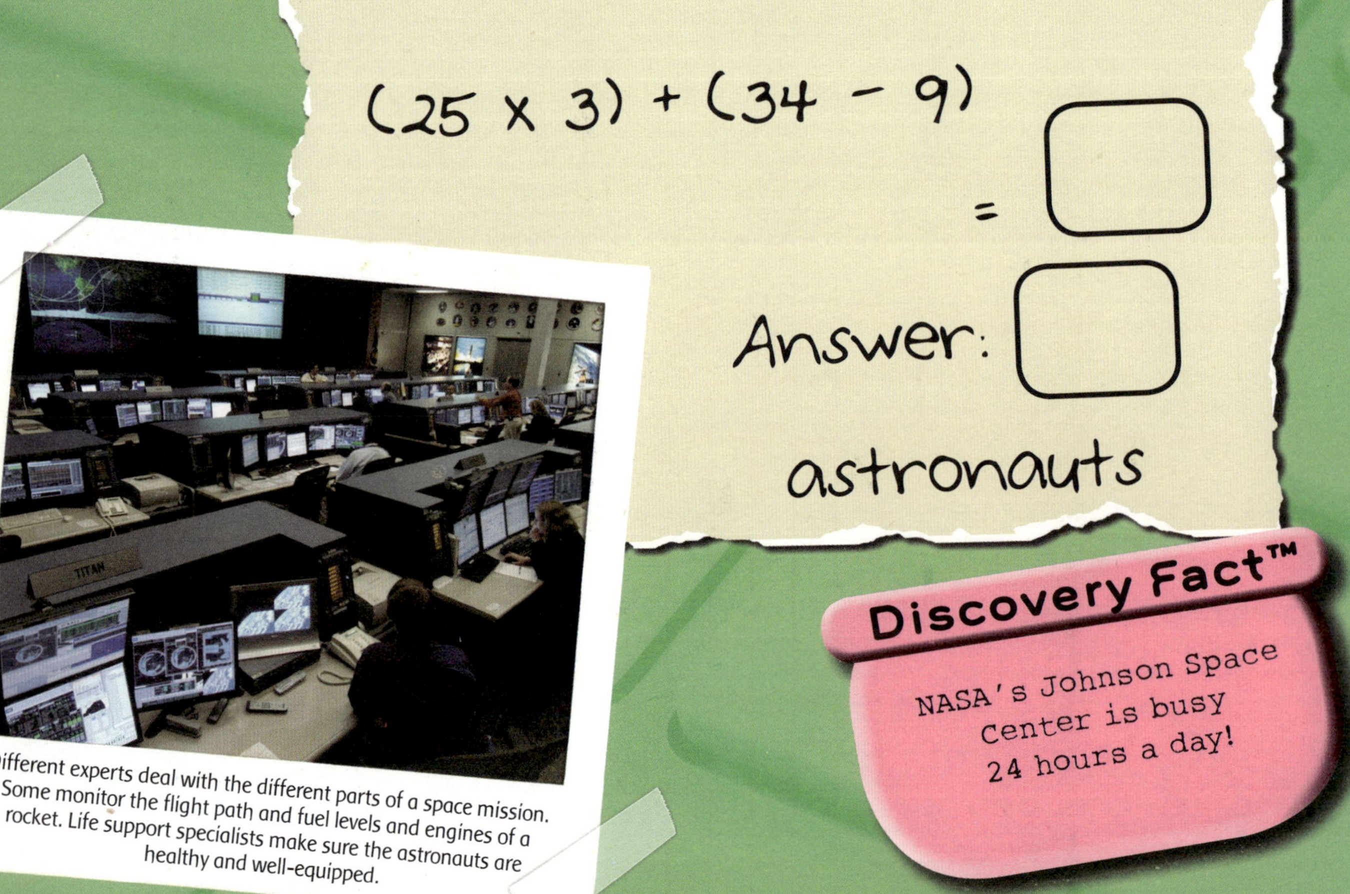

Different experts deal with the different parts of a space mission. Some monitor the flight path and fuel levels and engines of a rocket. Life support specialists make sure the astronauts are healthy and well-equipped.

Discovery Fact™

NASA's Johnson Space Center is busy 24 hours a day!

Answer: 100 astronauts (plus another 2,900 staff)

Launchpad!

Discovery Fact™

If there is ever a problem during liftoff, a rocket will do an emergency landing into the sea.

Check out this picture of the ESA rocket taking off. What do the letters ESA stand for? Unscramble the letters to find out!

reunopea

__ __ __ __ __ __ __ __

paces

__ __ __ __ __

acegny

__ __ __ __ __ __

The main launchpad for the ESA is at Kourou, French Guiana. It is near the equator, where the planet's spin is fastest. This gives rockets blasting off a good forward speed for their orbit.

Clue: The ESA is Europe's equivalent of NASA. (NASA stands for North American Space Agency.)

Answer: European Space Agency

Liftoff!

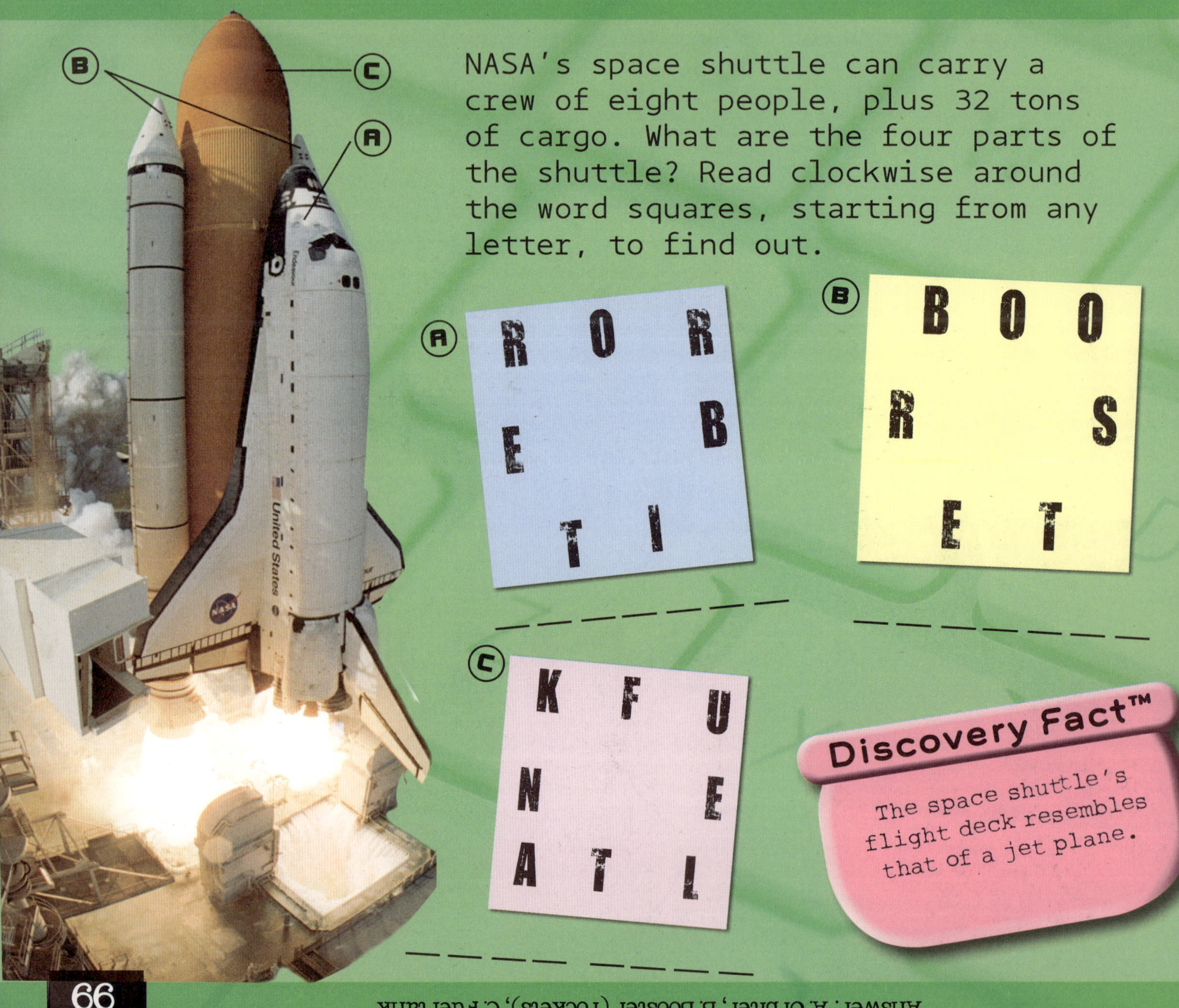

NASA's space shuttle can carry a crew of eight people, plus 32 tons of cargo. What are the four parts of the shuttle? Read clockwise around the word squares, starting from any letter, to find out.

A

R O R
E B
T I

_ _ _ _ _ _ _

B

B O O
R S
E T

_ _ _ _ _ _ _

C

K F U
N E
A T L

_ _ _ _   _ _ _ _

Discovery Fact™

The space shuttle's flight deck resembles that of a jet plane.

Answer: A Orbiter, B Booster (rockets), C Fuel tank

Mega Rockets!

Ariane rockets' boosters detach at a height of 41 miles and parachute into the sea.

Europe's main launchers are Ariane rockets. These two boosters help during the first few minutes of flight, when the fuel weight is at its heaviest and the pull of gravity at its strongest. Do you know how high and heavy the Ariane 5 boosters are? Do the math to find out!

A rocket such as the Ariane 5 burns fuel to make a blast of hot gases, like a continuous explosion, that carries it upward.

Answer: A. 194 feet tall, B. 944 tons (when fully fueled)

Space Day Trips!

In the future, it may be possible to take day trips to space. SpaceShipOne and SpaceShipTwo are two small space planes that can journey to space and back in one day. What year was SpaceShipOne launched into space: 2004 or 2005? The number which appears more often in the puzzle below is the answer.

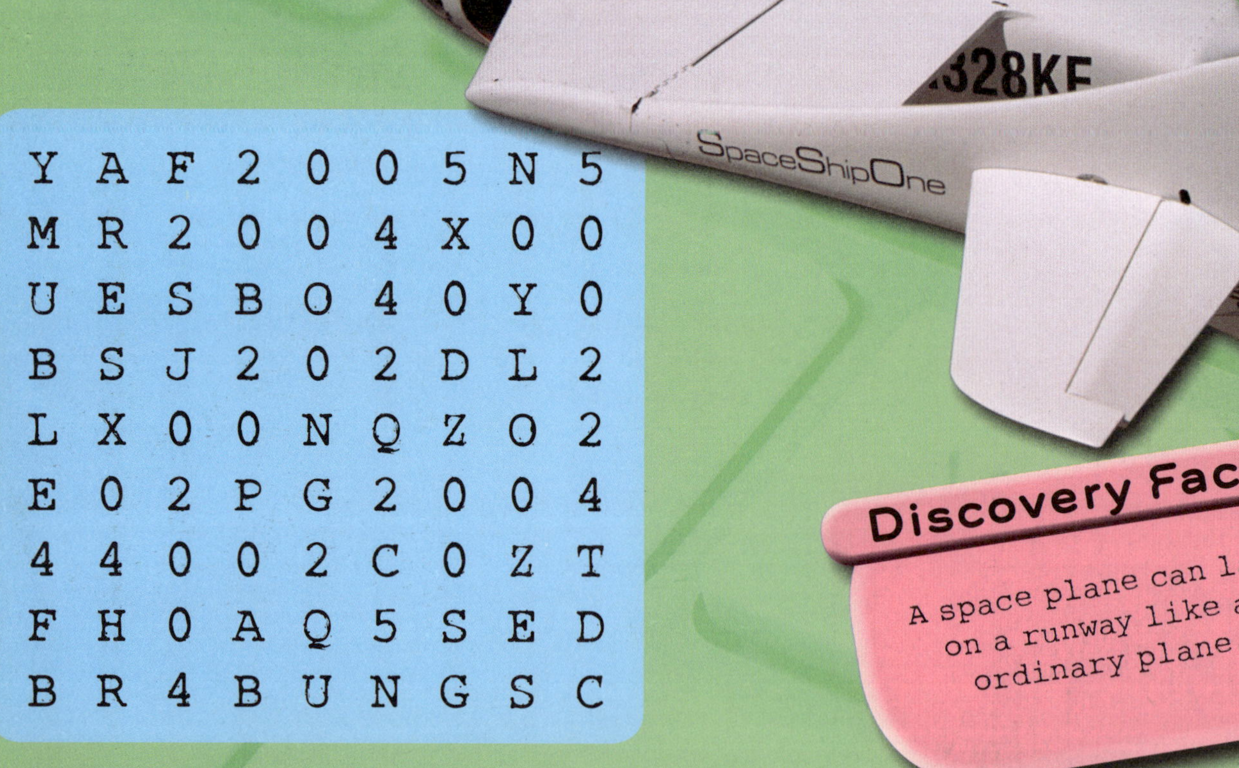

Y	A	F	2	0	0	5	N	5
M	R	2	0	0	4	X	0	0
U	E	S	B	O	4	0	Y	0
B	S	J	2	0	2	D	L	2
L	X	0	0	N	Q	Z	O	2
E	0	2	P	G	2	0	0	4
4	4	0	0	2	C	0	Z	T
F	H	0	A	Q	5	S	E	D
B	R	4	B	U	N	G	S	C

Discovery Fact™

A space plane can land on a runway like an ordinary plane.

Answer: 2004

International Space Station!

Since 1988, the International Space Station (ISS) has gradually been built. By what year should it be complete? Work your way through the maze to find out! When you find the exit, it will lead you to the correct answer.

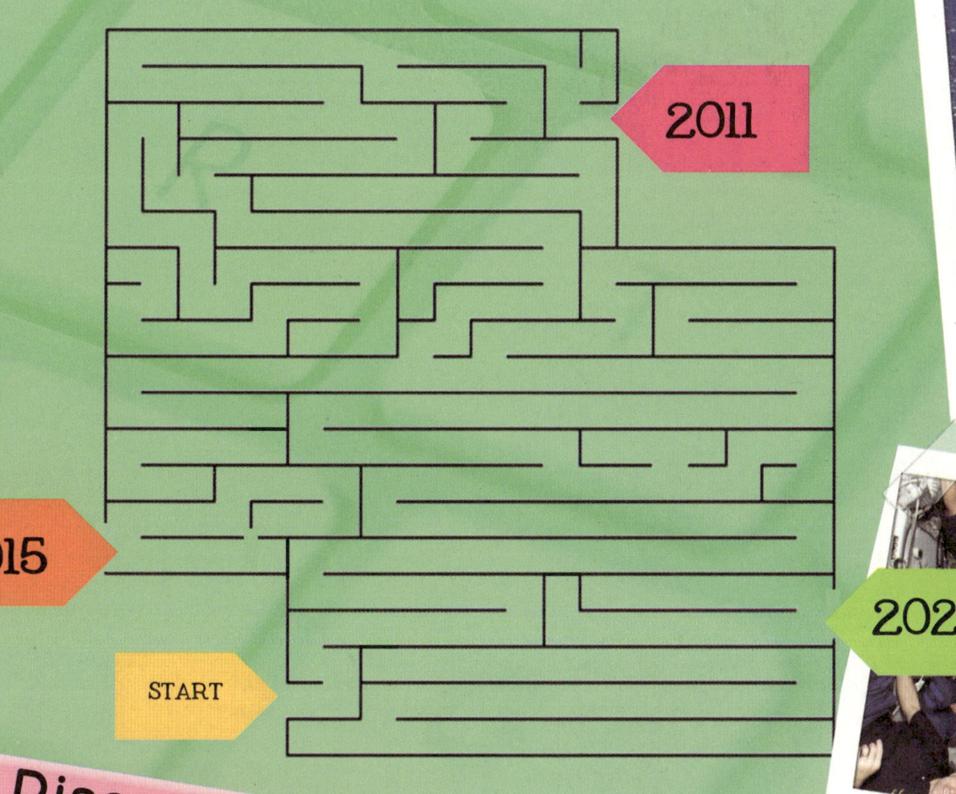

The ISS orbits Earth nearly 16 times each day.

Everything in the ISS is weightless and floats around if not secured.

Discovery Fact™

The International Space Station can sometimes be seen from Earth as a fast moving dot in the sky.

Answer: 2011

Mighty Mars!

Mars has been visited more than any other planet. Unscramble the letters below to discover the names of some of the spacecraft that have visited!

Jets of gas can be used to settle slowly onto the Martian surface.

(A) Oporttpuniy

_ _ _ _ _ _ _ _ _ _ _

(B) Phenixo

_ _ _ _ _ _ _

(C) Spitri

_ _ _ _ _ _

Discovery Fact™

Probes collect samples of Martian soil and rocks to see if there are traces of life there.

Answer: A Opportunity, B Phoenix (pictured), C Spirit

Around The World!

Discovery Fact™

An orbit is when an object or planet goes around another object in a circular or elliptical (oval) path.

What word do we use to refer to man-made craft orbiting Earth, other planets, or the Sun? Unscramble the letters to find out!

s t l e a e l t i

_ _ _ _ _ _ _ _ _

Launched in 2006, the two STEREO satellites orbit the Sun, taking images at the same time from millions of miles apart. Computers combine these into one three-dimensional image.

Each STEREO satellite is about 21 feet wide, including the solar panels. STEREO stands for Solar Terrestrial Relations Observatory.

Answer: Satellite

Payload!

A payload is what a rocket carries into space. From 2015, U.S. lunar missions will use different vehicles to transport crew and cargo. How much will the heavy cargo launch vehicle, powered by five shuttle engines and two boosters, lift? Do the math to find out.

The nose casings and the boosters of the heavy cargo launch vehicle fall away in orbit.

Discovery Fact™

A rocket booster can produce more than 200 decibels of noise!

Rocket Power!

Discovery Fact™

A receiver is a device that detects radio waves.

What is the fuel called that is used to power a rocket engine? Unscramble the letters to find out!

L T P E R
P N O A L

_ _ _ _ _ _ _ _ _ _

The Russian Soyuz rocket has four huge nozzles surrounded by smaller boosters.

Answer: Propellant

Moon Walk!

Since 1969, many astronauts have walked on the Moon. Do the math below to find out how many.

Answer: 12 astronauts have walked on the Moon.

Stardust!

A comet particle impact caught in aerogel.

The probe Stardust went on a 1.9-billion-mile trip to Comet Wild 2 to collect particles of dust, then returned to Earth's orbit to drop off its samples. But how big was the probe's particle collector? When you find the exit route, it will lead you to the correct answer.

Discovery Fact™

The Stardust probe's particle collector was made of aerogel, a soft, spongy substance almost as light as air.

START

The size of a tennis court.

The size of a baseball stadium.

The size of a tennis racket.

Answer: The size of a tennis racket.

Saturn Probe!

Among other things, the Cassini-Huygens probe discovered four new small moons of Saturn.

In October 1997, the probe Cassini-Huygens was launched on a mission to study Saturn. Do the math below to find out how many years it took the probe to get to its destination.

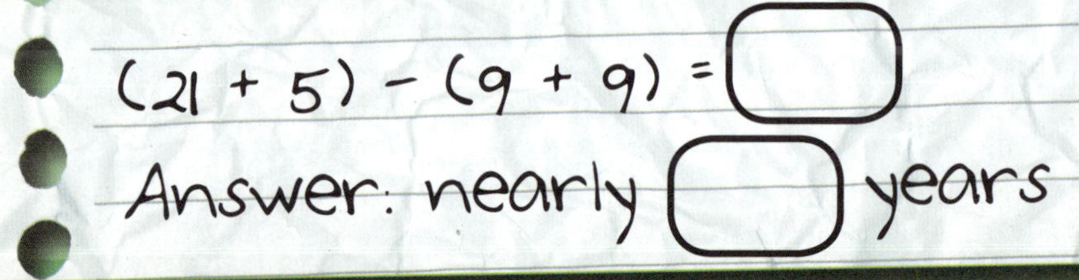

New Horizons!

The probe New Horizons (about the size of a full bed) took off in 2006 on an immense nine-and-a-half-year, 3.5-billion-mile journey to the most distant target of any probe so far. What was it aiming for? Read around this word circle to find out. The first letter of the word is the letter in the center.

__ __ __ __ __

Answer (top): Nearly 8 years
Answer (bottom): Pluto (a dwarf planet on the edge of our solar system)

Space Walk!

An astronaut's space suit is an amazing piece of life-support technology. How much do you think one costs? Do the math to find out.

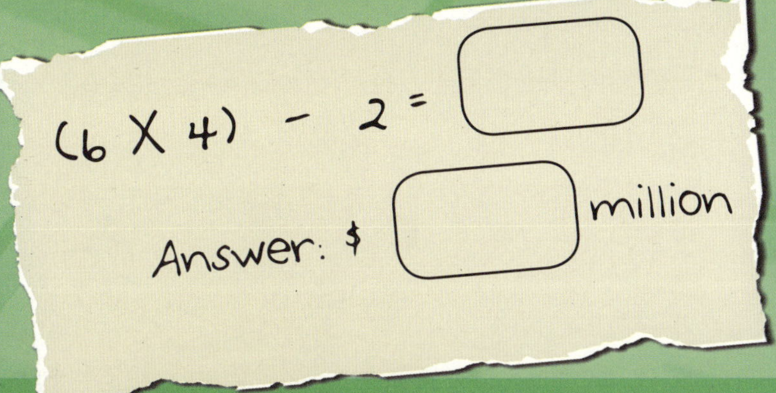

Astronauts have to wear a spacesuit every time they venture outside their craft.

Critical Gas!

A space suit pumps a very important gas to let the astronaut breathe. Read around the word circle below to find out what it is. The first letter of the word is the letter in the center of the circle.

_ _ _ _ _ _

Answer (top): $22 million Answer (bottom): Oxygen

Very Large Telescope!

The views of all the telescopes combined equal one telescope 52 feet across.

The Very Large Telescope (VLT) is formed of a number of telescopes designed to work together to produce one image. Do the math to find out some awesome facts.

A How many telescopes work together in the VLT?

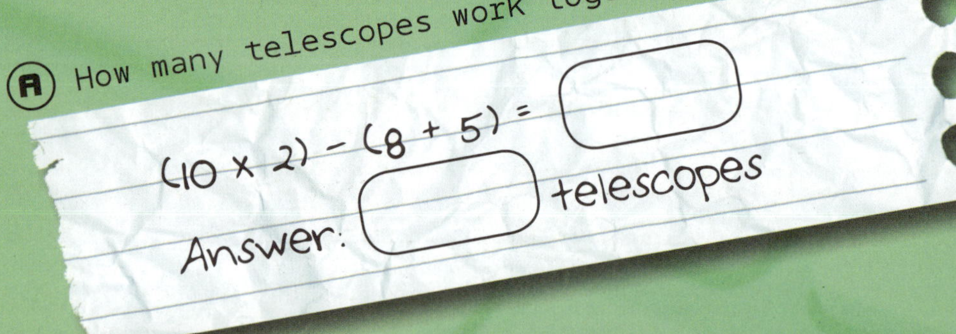

Discovery Fact

The smaller telescopes in the VLT can be moved to help "fill in" the scene.

B The VLT has a combination of smaller and larger telescopes. The smaller ones each have a mirror 6 feet across, but how wide are the mirrors on the four main telescopes?

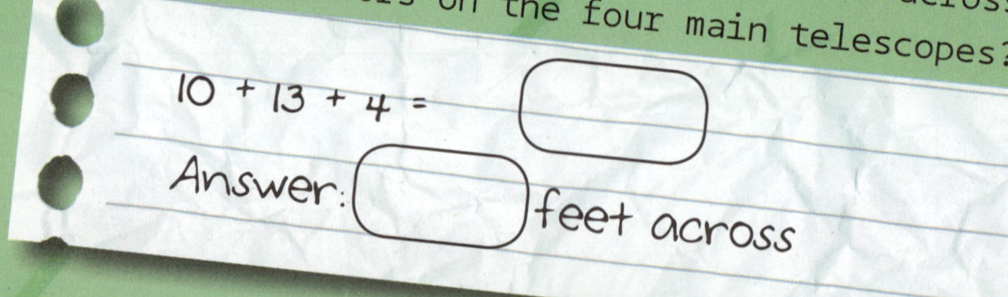

Answer: A. 7 telescopes, B. 27 feet across

VLT Site!

The VLT is situated 8,500 feet above sea level in the Atacama Desert. Here, the skies are clear about 350 nights a year, and there is no light, air pollution, or water vapor in the air to reduce the performance of the telescopes. What country is the Atacama Desert in? Solve the word square below to find out!

The VLT captured this image of spiral galaxy NGC 3190, which is 80 million light-years away, using a 14-minute exposure.

The VLT's mirrors are accurate to within a millionth of an inch. The mirrors are resurfaced every year.

Clue: It's a country in South America.

__ __ __ __ __

Discovery Fact™

The VLT can pick out objects that other telescopes cannot see—including planets going around other stars that may harbor life.

Answer: Chile

Strong Arm!

A German robot company called Kuka has built "Titan," the world's strongest robot arm. How heavy a weight can it actually move? Find your way through the maze below to find out. When you find the exit route, it will lead you to the correct answer.

Discovery Fact™

The "Titan" robot can move weights more than 10 feet in any direction using its five sets of joints.

Answer: 1 ton

Iris Scanning!

Discovery Fact™

Compared to fingerprints, iris scanning is less likely to cause a false match.

The iris is the colored part of the eye. No two eyes, even of the same person, have the same pattern. In iris scanning, a digital camera takes a detailed picture of the iris, which is analyzed by computer and converted into a digital pattern. But why is iris scanning so useful? Crack the code below to find out!

A picture of the iris is taken using infrared light in a digital camera, which can reveals more detail than normal light. It is quick and safe and works fine even if the person is wearing glasses or contact lenses.

z	y	x	w	v	u	t	s	r	q	p	o	n	m	l	k	j	i	h	g	f	e	d	c	b	a
a	b	c	d	e	f	g	h	i	j	k	l	m	n	o	p	q	r	s	t	u	v	w	x	y	z

z	o	n	l	h	g		r	n	k	l	h	h	r	y	o	v		g	l		u	z	p	v

Answer: Almost impossible to fake

Driverless Vehicle!

This modified Volkswagen Tuareg car has cameras, lasers, radar, and GPS. In 2005, it won the DARPA Grand Challenge, a competition for driverless cars sponsored by the Department of Defense. But what did its makers call the car? Unscramble the word circle to find out. The first letter of the word is the letter in the center of the circle.

__ __ __ __ __ __ __

Assembly Line!

Today's cars and trucks are made mostly by robots. Find out how many robots a typical assembly line fo[r] cars or trucks uses by solving the numbers below.

Discovery Fact™

Most factory robots are controlled by computers.

[Ans]wer (top): Stanley Answer (bottom): More than 500 robots

Wind Turbine!

Wind turbines turn the force of the wind into "green" electricity. How many average homes can be powered by a single large turbine? Do the math to find out!

1,700 − (2 x 150) = ☐

Answer: Over ☐ homes

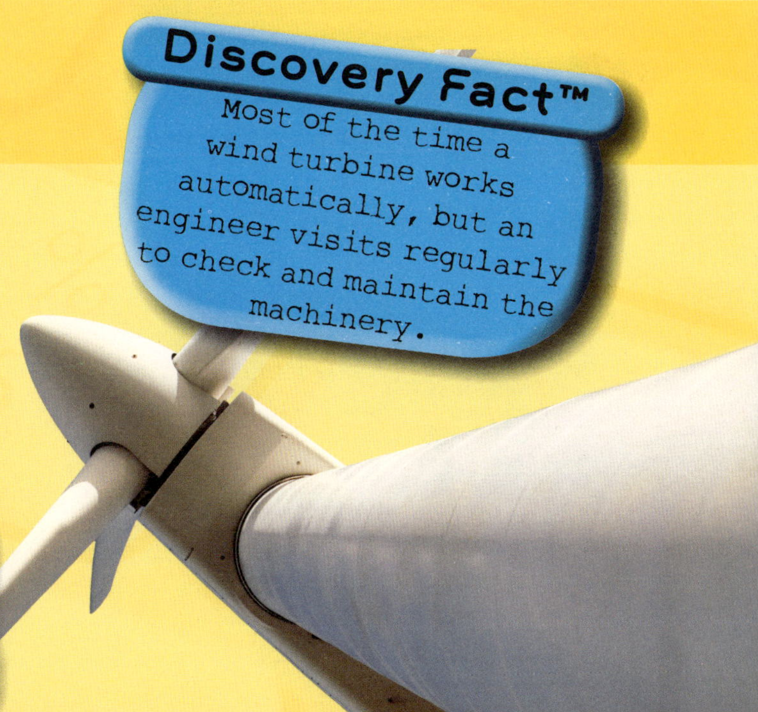

Discovery Fact™

Most of the time a wind turbine works automatically, but an engineer visits regularly to check and maintain the machinery.

Rotors!

The rotor blades on a wind turbine can twist on the shaft to change the angle at which they face the wind. When do you think they are angled almost on edge so that they do not spin too fast and topple the turbine? Unscramble the letters to find out!

ni gihh inwds

_ _ _ _ _ _ _ _ _ _ _

Answer (top): Over 1,400 homes   Answer (bottom): In high winds

Wind Farm!

Discovery Fact

The rotor blades on the largest wind turbines are almost 200 feet long.

Several wind turbines together are called a wind farm, and more and more of them are being built. Follow the lines to find out which of the facts below about wind farms are true, and which are false!

false

Ⓐ The wind cannot be guaranteed, so we also need other ways of making electricity.

Ⓑ Some people think that wind turbines are ugly

Ⓒ Wind power will never run out.

Ⓓ Wind provides free energy.

Ⓔ Wind turbines burn polluting fossil fuels.

Ⓕ Most people like the loud "whooshing" noises wind turbines make.

Answer: A True, B True, C True, D True, E False, F False

Power It Up!

This Danish power station makes electricity from natural gas.

Electricity is the world's favorite form of energy, and it powers many of the gadgets in this book. Our electricity is created in power stations and then fed into a huge network that takes the electricity to buildings. But what makes the electricity in the first place? Solve these word squares to discover three fossil fuels that are burned to generate electricity.

Ⓐ

___ ___ ___

Ⓑ
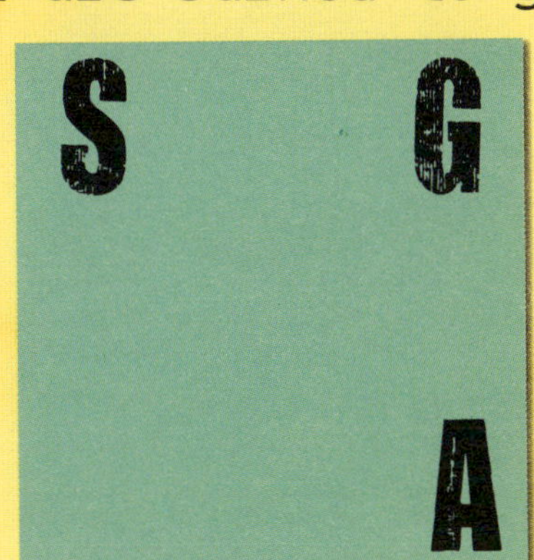

___ ___ ___

Ⓒ

___ ___ ___ ___

Discovery Fact™

Burning fossil fuels makes polluting fumes and speeds up global warming.

Answer: A Oil, B Gas, C Coal

Steam Turbines!

The turbines are checked carefully when the power station is taken "off line."

Most power stations use steam turbines to generate electricity. Follow the lines to discover how these work!

step 1.

step 2.

step 3.

step 4.

Ⓐ Spinning a wire in a strong magnetic field generates electricity.

Ⓑ The turbine is joined to a generator and spins its coils of wire in a strong magnetic field.

Ⓒ This blasts past the angled blades of a turbine to make it spin.

Ⓓ Burning fuel boils water into a high-pressure steam.

Discovery Fact™

All power stations feed their power into a huge network known as the grid.

Answer: Step 1, D; Step 2, C; Step 3, B; Step 4, A

Securitech!

Discovery Fact™

Gamma rays, normal X-rays, and backscatter X-rays, bounce back differently off different materials.

At an airport these days a special scanner may be used that can "see" under clothes to reveal hidden weapons. What rays do these scanners use? Find your way through the maze below to find out. When you find the exit route, it will lead you to the correct answer.

Answer: Backscatter X-rays

Facial Recognition!

Today's sophisticated facial recognition software uses a computer to store information about people's features. Any face picture can then be compared to a scan. Solve the word squares below to find three of the features that facial recognition software measures.

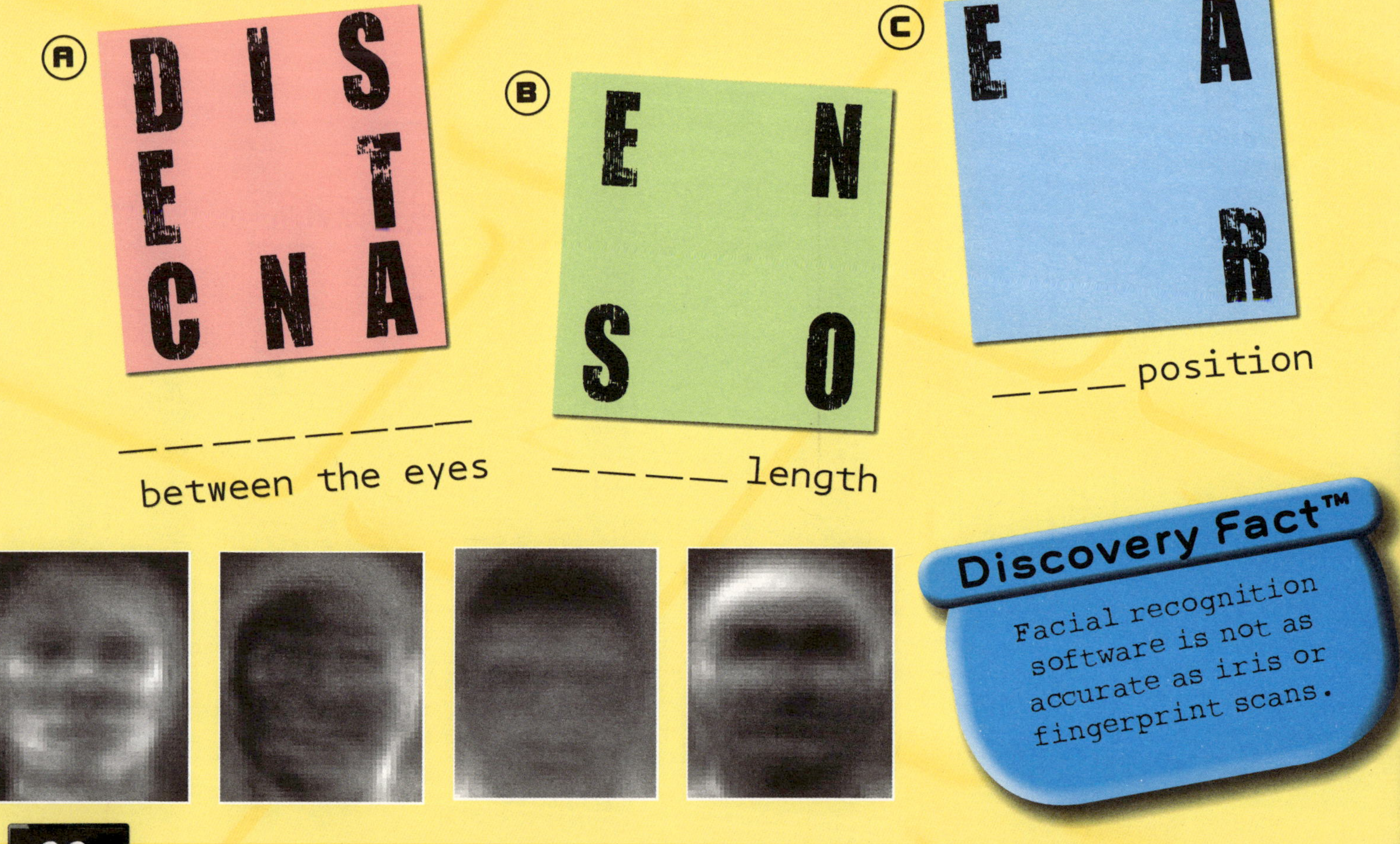

Answer: A Distance between the eyes, B Nose length, C Ear position

Top Technology!

In scientific research, laser beams are split, angled, and bounced back on a large work area called a laser optical bench.

Solve this word circle to discover the name of a type of technology essential to many of the gadgets in this book, including CD and DVD players. It was invented in 1960 and is high-intensity radiation emitted from a solid, liquid, or gaseous medium.

___ ___ ___ ___ ___

Artificial Star!

Discovery Fact™

Scientists measured the distance to the Moon by bouncing a laser off it.

Astronomers use a very powerful laser to make an "artificial star" in the night sky to help focus their telescopes. How high up into the night sky does this laser reach? Do the math below to find out.

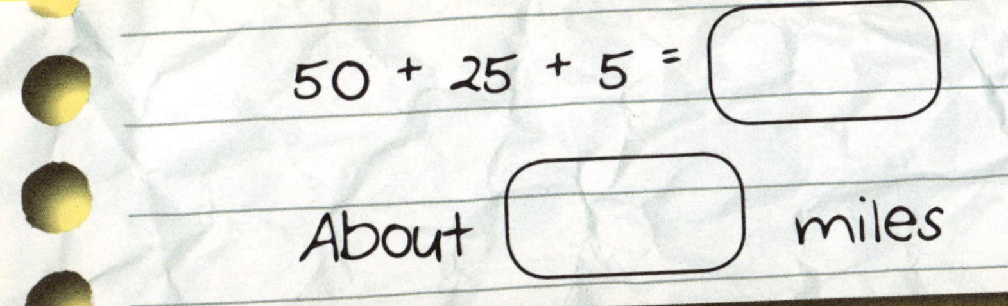

Answer (top): Laser   Answer (bottom): About 80 miles

Powerful!

Lasers emitted from the gas carbon dioxide have so much energy that they can melt what substance? Unscramble the letters below to find out!

a m e l t

_____ _____ _____ _____ _____

This man is testing a laser range finder (distance measurer) for a weapon.

Staying Safe!

Safety is vital when testing high-power lasers. What should you always wear over your eyes? Read around this word circle to find out. The first letter of the word is the letter in the center of the circle.

_____ _____ _____ _____ _____ _____ _____

Discovery Fact™

The most delicate lasers are used to make microchips containing parts thousands of times smaller than this period.

Answer (top): Metal   Answer (bottom): Goggles

Securitech!

Discovery Fact™

RFID tags have been put under people's skin as an experiment, so they can pass security barriers.

There are billions of RFID tags in the world and you probably use them every day without even realizing it. An RFID tag is an electronic gadget that transmits radio waves about its identity in response to radio waves it receives. Many types of smart cards use RFID tags. Crack the code below to find out what RFID means!

z	y	x	w	v	u	t	s	r	q	p	o	n	m	l	k	j	i	h	g	f	e	d	c	b	a
a	b	c	d	e	f	g	h	i	j	k	l	m	n	o	p	q	r	s	t	u	v	w	x	y	z

i	z	w	r	l		u	i	v	j	f	v	m	x	b

r	w	v	m	g	r	u	r	x	z	g	r	l	m

w	v	e	r	x	v

The Oyster card is used for transportation in London, UK, instead of tickets. It uses an RFID tag.

Answer: Radio frequency identification device

Three-Dimensional Printer!

The pages in this book are printed on a flat, two-dimensional surface. Three-dimensional printing adds depth to produce a solid object. This brand-new technology can "print" all kinds of items, from plastic toys to complex, working machines. Follow the lines below to find out how it works!

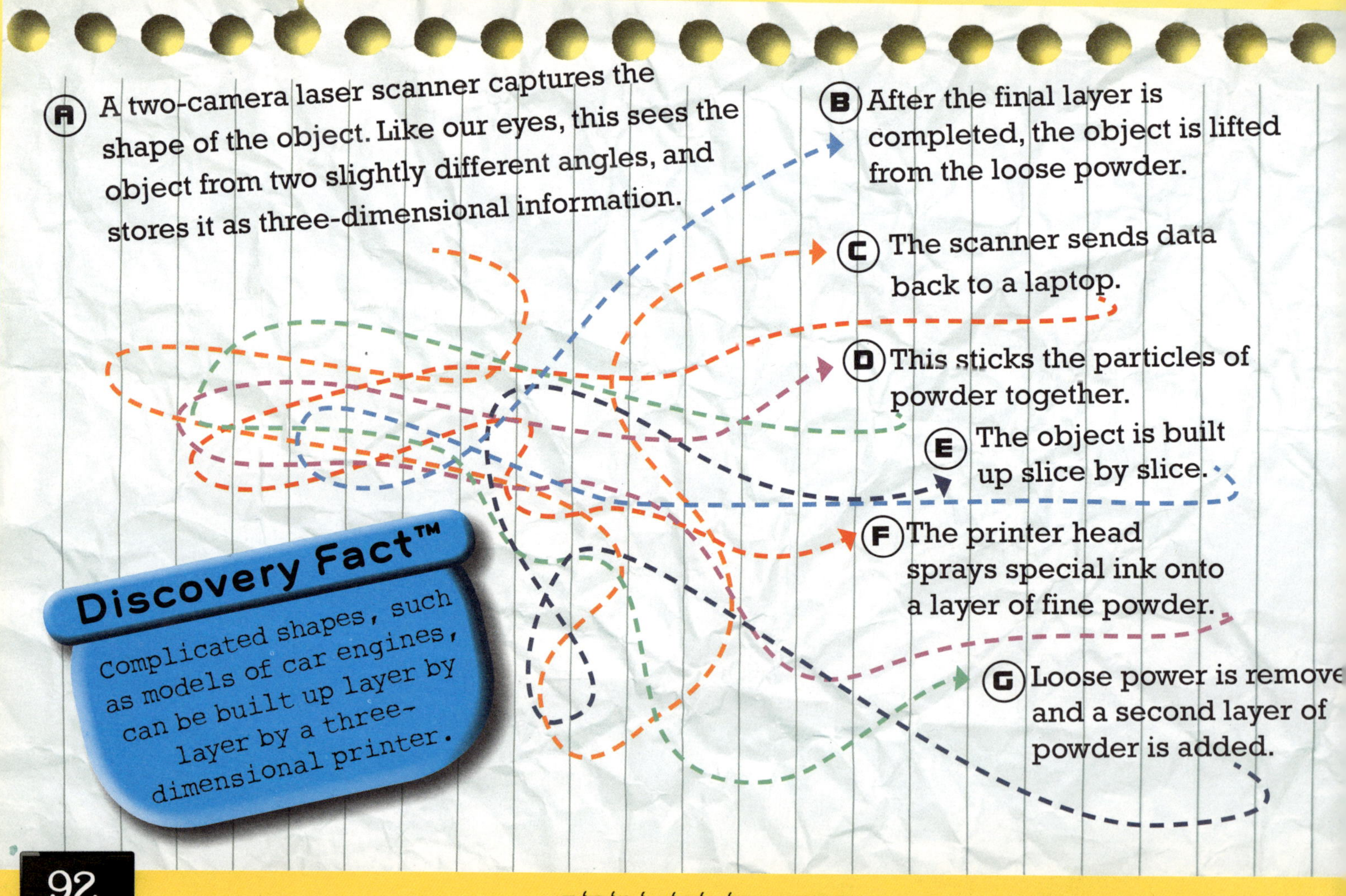

Answer: A, C, F, D, G, E, B

Nanotechnology!

Discovery Fact™

Nanotechnology deals with particles less than 100 nanometers wide.

"Nano" is not just small, or even microscopic, it's even smaller than that. Cool new nanotechnology builds objects and machines at the scale of individual atoms and molecules. In the word puzzle below are three everyday objects that have been improved through nanotechnology. Can you find them all?

A	L	U	W	E	E	J	G	G	R	V
S	U	N	S	C	R	E	E	N	S	O
H	S	O	B	Y	Q	D	U	S	Z	C
X	E	Q	D	N	I	F	K	W	R	K
O	H	Y	S	Z	C	A	A	P	A	W
J	T	P	U	E	M	E	N	W	K	Z
E	O	Z	S	Q	V	N	Q	C	W	U
S	L	L	A	B	S	I	N	N	E	T
Y	C	G	S	G	N	C	F	F	G	X
P	U	E	K	A	M	A	N	E	M	M
U	I	A	G	E	H	O	G	E	C	N

Answer: Sunscreen, tennis balls, makeup

Discovery Fact™

Carbon is very useful in nanotechnology because its atoms can join together in many different patterns.

Nanoman!

"Nanoman" was built by researchers from Birmingham University, England, from individual carbon atoms. He stands 400 nanometers tall. How many of them standing on each other's heads would be as tall as this letter "I?" Do the math below to find out!

20,000 − (5,000 × 2) =

Answer:

Bar Code Basics!

Bar codes are found on all kinds of products and packaging (including this book). A laser scans the bar code to identify the product. What do you think the different lines in the bar code on this book represent? Unscramble the letters to find out!

__ __ __ __ __ __ __

Discovery Fact™

Bar code information scanned in by a laser is fed to a computer, which interprets the data.

Answer (top): 10,000 Answer (bottom): Numbers

Agromachine!

Discovery Fact™

A modern combine harvester's onboard GPS displays maps of the field, showing how much is left to harvest.

Combine harvesters have been around for about 180 years, but today onboard technology allows the latest agro-machines to harvest farmland faster and more efficiently than ever before. What do you think a farmer these days uses to decide which areas to harvest? When you find the exit route, it will lead you to the correct answer!

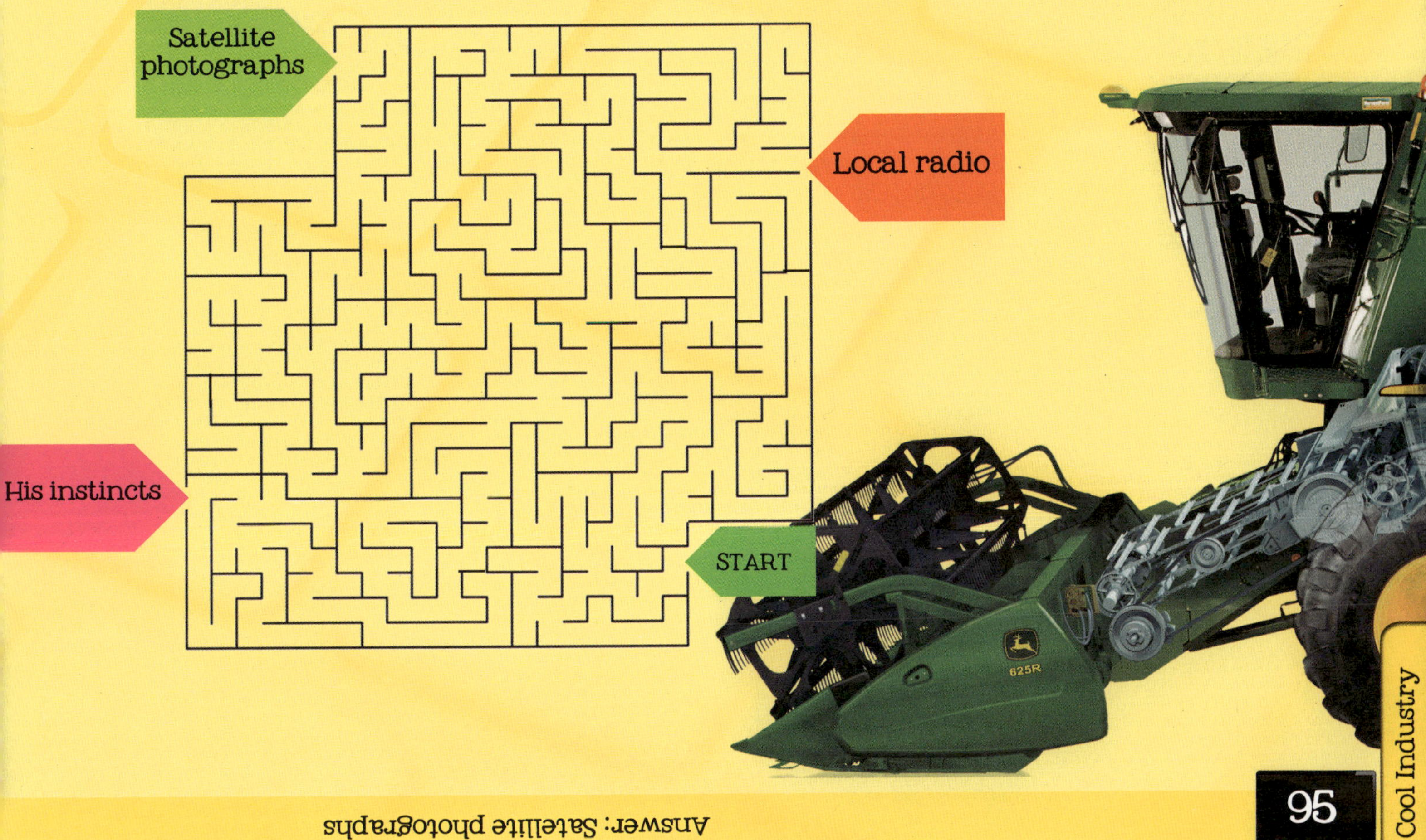

Answer: Satellite photographs

Acknowledgments

Front cover: bl Wow Wee Toys, bc Nintendo, br Wikipedia
Back cover: c Dreamstime.com/Steve Mitchell

All artwork supplied by The Apple Agency Ltd (apple.co.uk)

1 Kawasaki, 2 tl Nintendo, 2 tr Monte Cristo, 2 b Wow Wee Toys, 5 tr Wikipedia, 5 bl Canon, 6 tr JVC, 6 bl Dreamstime.com/Ghubonamin, 7 Wikipedia, 8 Dreamstime.com/Steve Mitchell, 9 Monte Cristo, 10 Iophoto/dreamstime.com, 12 Wikipedia, 13 t Dreamstime.com/Andresr, 13 b Andyd/istockphoto.com, 14 Dreamstime.com/Dmitriy Aseev, 15 Dreamstime.com/Aleksandar Jocic, 16 tr Dreamstime.com, 16 b Roberts, 18 Nintendo, 19 Nintendo, 20 Nintendo, 21 Dreamstime.com, 23 Piercy Connor Ltd, 24 c Reuters/Corbis, 24 br Viatek, 25 Dyson, 26 t Nokia, 26 bl Dreamstime.com, 26 bc Wikipedia, 27 bl Dreamstime.com, 28 iRobot, 29 Wow Wee Toys, 30 Bugatti, 31 tr Kawasaki, 31 br moodboard/Corbis 32 b Dreamstime.com/Daniel Boiteau, 33 P1 Power Boat, 34 Stephen Frink/zefa/Corbis, 35 Wikipedia, 36 Magellan, 38 Kawasaki, 39 L. Tong/NewSport/Corbis, 40 Adidas, 41 Suunto, 42 front Silvershooter/istockphotocom, 42 background PLAINVIEW/istockphoto.com, 43 c Dreamstime.com, 43 tr Oliver Furrer/Brand X/Corbis, 44 Adidas, 45 Suunto, 46 technotr/istockphoto.com, 47 Gore-Tex, 48 Adidas, 49 Dreamstime.com, 50 Tim de Waele/Corbis, 51 Dreamstime.com, 52 Schlegelmilch/Corbis, 53 Seiko/Reuters/Corbis, 54 Pixland/Corbis, 55 iStock, 56 Dreamstime.com, 57 Alessandro Di Meo/epa/Corbis, 59 EndoWrist, 60 Dreamstime.com/Billyfoto, 61 Tony Savino/Corbis, 62 Dreamstime.com, 63 iStock, 64 Wikipedia, 65 ESA, 66 NASA, 67 ESA, 68 Jim Sugar/Corbis, 69 NASA, 70 NASA, 71 SOHO, 72 NASA, 73 Wikipedia, 74 NASA, 75 NASA, 76 t NASA, 76 b NASA, 77 NASA, 78 European Southern Observatory, 79 European Southern Observatory, 80 KUKA, 81 Wikipedia, 82 b Frederic Pitchal/Sygma/Corbis, 83 t istockphoto, 83 b Greg Smith/Corbis, 84 Dreamstime.com/Kamil Sobocki, 85 Dreamstime.com/Jean Schweitzer, 86 Wikipedia, 87 Dreamstime.com/Stephen Sweet, 89 tr Charles O'Rear/Corbis, 90 Wikipedia, 91 br TFL, 93 tr Dreamstime.com/Yurii Gorul'ko, 93 bl Dreamstime.com/Vitaly Valua, 94 R. E. Palmer Birmingham University, 95 John Deere